# Don't Call
## the THRIFT SHOP

# Don't Call
# the THRIFT SHOP

## What to Do with a Lifetime of Well–Loved Possessions

*SUSANNAH RYDER*

M. Evans
Lanham • New York • Boulder • Toronto • Plymouth, UK

Published by M. Evans
An imprint of The Rowman & Littlefield Publishing Group, Inc.
4501 Forbes Boulevard, Suite 200, Lanham, Maryland 20706

Estover Road, Plymouth PL6 7PY, United Kingdom

Distributed by National Book Network

**Library of Congress Cataloging-in-Publication Data**

Ryder, Susannah,
    Don't call the thrift shop : what to do with a lifetime of well-loved possessions / Susannah Ryder.
        p.   cm.
    Includes index.
    ISBN-10: 1-59077-111-7 (pbk. : alk. paper)
    ISBN-13: 978-1-59077-111-2 (pbk. : alk. paper)
    1. Collectibles—United States—Marketing.   2. Antiques—United States—Marketing.   I. Title.
    NK1125.R93 2007
    790.1'32—dc22

                                                                2006008547

⊗™ The paper used in this publication meets the minimum requirements of American National Standard for Information Sciences—Permanence of Paper for Printed Library Materials, ANSI/NISO Z39.48–1992.

Manufactured in the United States of America.

# CONTENTS

# ACKNOWLEDGMENTS
# AND THANKS

This book is dedicated to my friend, mentor, and advisor, Norine Dresser, for her invaluable support, and to P. J. Dempsey, who gave me the opportunity to write this book.

Special thanks to the following individuals and organizations for their contributions and materials: Sidney Adair; Mary Cullather; Seth Bright; Jim Bergman; Bruno Corsini; Kim Daniels; John Dugan; Mark C. Grove; Viga Hall; Frank Hettig; Elayne Horton; Don Jones; Tom La Forge; Ann Molod; Janet Murillo; Trudie Pansey; Marc Richards; Susan Romaine, CFP; Paul Romero; Paul Thompson, G. G., ASA; A. J. Mawer; Raymond Scott; Sandra Tropper, ASA; James Wagner, CFP; Michael Walsh; Sharon Yost.

I would also like to thank:

- Anne Kern, Certified Financial Planning Board of Standards
- Betsy Snyder, American Society of Appraisers
- Rick Wolf, Sotheby's
- Joe Orlando, Professional Sports Authenticators
- David Hall, Professional Coin Grading Services

- David Hertsgaard, Eames Office
- Mike Van Eaton, Van Eaton Galleries
- Ruth Feldman, The Doll Shoppe
- Arnold Blumberg, Gemstone Publishing
- Cheryl Marks, Cheryl Marks Estate Services

and *American Art Review*, *Antiques and the Arts*, Antiques and Fine Art, *Art and Antiques Magazine*, AntiqueDress.com, AskArt, J.C. Ames Auctioneers, Bonhams & Butterfields, Coinfacts, Chard, Christie's, Diamond Galleries, Heritage Galleries, Julian's Vintage Clothing, *Maine Antiques Digest*, Sotheby's, Skinner's, Swann's, Superior Galleries, Treadway Gallery, Vintage Vixen, PCGS, Kitco, Rago Arts, and Replacements.

Thanks to Jed Lyons, Rick Rinehart, Dulcie Wilcox, April Leo, and the wonderful team at M. Evans/Rowman & Littlefield Publishers.

# INTRODUCTION: WHY THIS BOOK?

O ver the years, in my work as a financial advisor, I would often meet people with piles of stock certificates, old statements, papers, checks, and a bewildering array of letters and correspondence from financial institutions. I would find out there was a death in the family or some other need to take a "financial inventory." I would help my clients sort through these mystifying documents, evaluate and appraise their holdings, organize and understand their financial assets, and decide how to manage their investments.

Then, a few years ago, I served as the executor of a family estate. What a confusing process it was! I had experience selling fine art and antiques, yet I was lost when it came to Oriental rugs, stamps, wrist watches, and rare books. I realized I was much like my own clients who came to me for help—I didn't know what I should keep or sell, how much anything was worth, how things could be sold, and where exactly to turn for professional help.

Soon I found that the world of antiques and collectibles had changed dramatically. Information once found only in libraries was now available at the click of a mouse. Online retailers offered rare objects that once could be purchased only at exclusive shops. EBay had created a more liquid market for millions of collectibles. Third-party grading was emerging as an important factor in valuations. Fine art values were skyrocketing. All sorts of fun and interesting objects—some of which might seem unremarkable to the uneducated eye—were finding their way into collections and into the auction record books.

Almost every individual and family will encounter situations that raise the need to go through a houseful of family possessions and heirlooms. A move to a retirement home, an illness, a need for liquidity to meet expenses, a death in the family—these are often times of upheaval. It became clear to me that a guidebook was necessary—a roadmap for navigating the process of investigating, valuing, and selling many different kinds of personal property.

But there was no such book! So I decided I would write one, to share with others what I had learned, and to explore the exciting new world of resources changing and shaping new markets in antiques and collectibles.

Once I started the project, I learned very quickly that it would take many books, or many hundreds of books, to provide all the information necessary to complete an expert evaluation of any collection. I have tried to shed some light on the many reference sources that do exist, and to explain a little about how to work with the different professionals who are part of the process. The estate planning attorney, appraiser, auction company, antique dealer, art expert, tax advisor, liquidator, eBay assistant, and charitable institution all may have a role to play in your personal property decisions.

This book is intended only as a starting point, hopefully a compass to many of the valuable places where you will find people with knowledge and expertise far beyond my own. Please enjoy the journey. Have fun with your collections, learn from them, and let them change your lives.

# Don't Call
# the THRIFT SHOP

# 1

# LIFE STORIES

Patty's mother, Edna, was in her eighties. She had been widowed for nearly twenty years, and lived alone in the rambling house Patty had been raised in. Edna's health seemed good, and she was proud to be able to care for herself in her own home. It was a beautiful turn of the century house in rural Ohio, filled with old furniture, books, paintings, and china.

Patty's cousin Stacie often fretted to her about Edna.

"What will you do, when things change?" she would ask. "You live over two hundred miles away and you're busy with your kids. Aunt Edna needs to move closer to you. How will she manage a big house like this if her health starts to fail?"

"Stacie, she is so stubborn. I've tried to talk to her about . . . eventualities. She won't consider moving. She feels fine. I've looked at retirement facilities, and even talked to her about moving in with us, but she won't listen to any discussion. I know something will have to be done sooner or later. Jim has been saying the same thing. I don't know what to do . . . not yet, anyway."

Soon Edna's physical capabilities began to diminish. She suffered a series of small strokes. Patty was consumed with the process of finding home care, then a nursing home. Medical bills mounted. Her husband Jim and her young children also needed her time and attention.

Patty felt overloaded. When Edna passed away the next year, she was devastated. The end had come so suddenly. She was sure now that it had been wrong to allow her mother to live alone for so many years. They should have had more time together. She should have somehow insisted on it.

An attorney in Edna's neighborhood helped Patty administer Edna's estate. Many realtors called with offers for the house before it was even on the market. Jim urged her to sell the house quickly, before the real estate market cooled. Patty was flung into the process of negotiations, of multiple offers that were higher than she had ever imagined for the old house. Soon it would be time to begin moving Edna's numerous belongings so the new owners could move in. But what should she do with her mother's things? Patty and Jim's own home was already filled with furniture. She had nowhere to store fragile, breakable items in a house with young children.

Patty found the process of sorting through her mother's things unbearable. There were so many memories in the house! She was unprepared for the physical and emotional task of moving. Sorting through her mother's personal papers, bank statements, insurance policies, and letters had been enough of an ordeal for her. She took home her mother's jewelry, and a few other special mementos. There seemed to be hundreds of pieces of china and glassware, heavy mahogany furniture, lamps, vases, paintings, and prints. In the attic sat boxes of Patty's old dolls, toys, books from her childhood, clothes from several decades, and more furniture. There were even old tools and fishing gear in the garage that had belonged to her father.

Stacie came over to help her spend several days packing items and making decisions.

"Stacie, I just can't cope with all this right now."

"Maybe you should put these things in storage."

Patty considered this. Paying a storage bill, then having to come back and sort through things later. . . . She wasn't even sure if her mother's household articles were worth anything. The attorney handling the real estate sale phoned. The buyer was asking when the house would be ready.

"I don't know . . . we have to decide what to do with the furniture and other things," Patty told him. "I just don't know how long it will be. . . ."

The attorney called again a few hours later. He had discussed the situation with the buyer, who had offered to add five thousand dollars to the home purchase for a list of contents he would prepare.

Patty felt immediately relieved. "That would be a perfect solution! I can keep some of Mother's personal belongings, things that I would like to give the children, and he can have all this other stuff."

Stacie was uncertain. "Shouldn't you have the furniture appraised? And the paintings? What about the china? Don't you want to keep it?"

"I'll keep a few pieces that I know she liked. But I have no room for most of this, and Jim likes modern things."

"But what if these things are worth more than what he's offering?"

"Stacie, maybe they are. We're getting a fantastic price for the house, more than I could ever have imagined. Mother enjoyed these things while she lived here. Perhaps it's best that the furniture should stay with the house. Maybe she would have liked that."

Patty told the attorney she would accept the buyer's offer. She felt an enormous weight lift off her shoulders. She took home her mother's jewelry, and a few other special mementos, packed a few pieces of silver and china to save, feeling she had made the right decision.

The new buyer of Edna's home listened to the attorney's news and mumured an unemotional reply. Inside, he was thrilled beyond belief. The antiques, American paintings, and Brilliant period cut glass alone were worth a small fortune at auction . . . and many things would appreciate in value even more in years to come.

Jill was a financial advisor. Her client, Marvin, an elderly retiree, had worked in the movie industry as a successful professional cinematographer. Jill would occasionally visit Marvin's home and go over his finances with him. She was aware that Marvin was a widower with no children, and that his nephew Charles, from Chicago, was Marvin's heir and would eventually be executor of his estate.

Marvin enjoyed his meetings with Jill. She asked questions about his career, but he liked best to reminisce about his days as a young artist, his marriage to a young French model, and the years they had spent in Paris socializing with artists and writers, at parties and salons, talking literature and politics with some of the most celebrated figures of the times.

Marvin was proud of his collection of early photographs, and Jill also noticed several pieces of art on the walls of Marvin's study. She had taken art history in college, and from what Marvin had told her of his past, she realized that the signed Picasso charcoal drawings, Raoul Dufy watercolors, and early Toulouse-Lautrec prints were undoubtedly authentic.

"Marvin, have you had these collections appraised?" Jill asked one day. "These Picassos—they're originals. And the photographs—some of them might be important, and valuable."

"I'm leaving all the photographs to the Film Institute," Marvin told her. "I've made a special gift of them in my will. They will be in good hands there."

Marvin's health eventually declined, and Charles arrived from Chicago to supervise his move to an assisted living facility. Jill was very sad to hear from him a few months later, telling her that Marvin had passed away peacefully.

"All the financial assets are in order," Jill told Charles when he called her again to initiate the estate transfer of Marvin's brokerage accounts. "But, Charles, I feel I must mention this—are you aware of the value of some of Marvin's collections? The art?"

"I'm taking the photography collection over to the Film Institute, if that's what you mean. They are going to honor Marvin with a permanent exhibit and a retrospective of his films. I'll make sure you're invited to the opening."

"There are also some pieces of art, in the study, that you should definitely have appraised."

"I'll do that."

One day a large sum of money was wired into Marvin's estate account, and Jill knew the house had been sold. Charles called again to notify Jill that he was transferring the account to his own financial advisor in Chicago. He thanked her for her long assistance to Marvin.

"Charles, did you ever get the art appraised?"

"Oh, you know, a man came over and appraised everything and gave me a check for everything that was in the house. He gave me fifteen thousand dollars for those pictures you mentioned. It was good you told me about it."

Jill drew in her breath and said nothing. The pieces were worth conservatively more than ten times what the liquidator had paid Charles. But it was over and done with, and Charles had received a tidy inheritance as it was. There was nothing she could do about it.

Sarah's uncle, Joe passed away after a long illness. A widower for many years, Joe had only one son. Sarah's cousin Ben had been born with cerebral palsy, and required special care as an adult. Sarah and the rest of Joe's relatives assumed that Joe's substantial estate would be left in trust to provide for Ben.

Sarah was surprised one day to hear from Joe's attorney. She learned that Joe had carefully planned for the cost of Ben's future care, and had been able to make substantial bequests to charities and gifts to other family members. To Sarah, he had left his book collection.

"He states in his will that you always loved to read," the attorney told her.

Sarah was overwhelmed by the news. She remembered years of visiting Uncle Joe and playing on the floor of his library, the walls dark with leather and gilt bindings. She was also dismayed—she lived in a small apartment on a teacher's salary. Where would she store so many books?

Sarah arranged to visit Joe's house to pick up the books. The real estate agent handling the sale of the house let her in. In a state of awe and dismay, Sarah found there were several hundred books in the library. Many of them were the leather and gilt-edged volumes she remembered, but there were also old books she had never looked at closely—many famous novels, their jackets covered with plastic covers, art, history, and illustrated books. What was she going to do with them all? How could she pack and move them? The trunk of her compact car would only hold a couple of boxes. Sarah felt disheartened. She phoned the attorney back and told him she would need more time to arrange the move.

"I don't know what to do. I don't have room for them all. I was thinking possibly I could try to sell some of them."

"Well, I can refer you to a local book dealer who purchases estates if you decide to."

"Let me think about it—that may be a good idea."

At the high school where she taught, Sarah sought out her friend John, a fellow English teacher, and told him of her dilemma. He asked her several questions about the books, surprising Sarah with his interest and knowledge.

"Are there any first editions? Signed or limited editions?"

"I don't really know. He had most of them for years and years. All I know is, I don't know where I'm going to keep them. Maybe I should try to sell some of them."

"Not without finding out more about them first. I'll help you. We can store some at my house or here at the school library if you run out of room—there's a storage room with a lock and key."

Sarah was amazed as John helped her take charge of the situation. He organized several students from the football team to help them pack the books carefully in clean cartons. They came to Sarah's small apartment with boards and cinder blocks to build makeshift bookshelves from the floor to the ceiling. John and the students borrowed a truck to move the boxes and the shelves were filled. Sarah was thrilled and surprised to see her apartment slowly take on a little of the look of her uncle's library.

John suggested Sarah make a catalog of the books. One Saturday afternoon, he came over to help her look at the books' first few pages and make descriptive notes about the titles and copyrights.

"I'm going to try to find out what some of these first editions and nineteenth-century things are worth," he told her. "They could be quite valuable. Your uncle was a very astute collector."

"How valuable?" Sarah had never heard of first editions or rare books. To her, books were something to study, to read and enjoy. "How can you find these things out?"

"I'm not sure but I'm going to try a few ideas."

John went to the school library and pored through a bibliographic catalog. He spent some time on the computer searching websites, not knowing at first what he was looking for. He browsed through the inventories of rare book dealers and found some companies he had never heard of, which conducted book auctions. All of it sounded very fascinating. Collectors seemed to be paying vast sums for certain important books. Why some were more valuable than others was not explained anywhere.

John paid a visit to a local book dealer and asked questions about the books in the dealer's shop. He told Sarah to look for a copy of a rare book price guide on a used book website he had found. Slowly, they began to identify many of the books in the collection and establish a range of prices some of them had been selling for at auctions and at rare book shops.

Eventually, Sarah consigned a few of her books to one of the rare book auction companies John had located. With the proceeds, she was able to make a down payment on a condo, with more room for shelves and an extra bedroom for her new library. She made a gift to John of a couple of volumes she thought would be of interest to him, but he had begun to frequent used book stores and estate sales, turning up with out-of-the-way literary items by beat poets and other writers Sarah had never heard of.

"You're starting your own collection!"

"I'm collecting the rare books of the future . . . at least, I hope so!"

On the anniversary of Joe's death, Sarah reflected on the major changes in her life that a seemingly small inheritance had brought. Her uncle could not have imagined the internet and all the knowledge she had been able to acquire in a short time. But she and John had both discovered a new world which brought them more than just financial reward, and she knew her uncle would have been pleased.

Every day, thousands of stories like these are unfolding, all with different outcomes. But the basic question is the same: when a move, an illness, a death, or a different unexpected life change occurs, what should we do with a lifetime of well-loved family possessions and heirlooms? There is not always time to study and evaluate furniture, art, antiques, and other collectibles that might be packed away in closets, attics, and desk drawers. Emotions at these times can take center stage, and, as Patty felt, it is not always the right time to be focusing on financial aspects of the situation.

## PLANNING AHEAD

What can we do to be better prepared?

Having Edna's belongings *appraised* or evaluated before her illness occurred might have helped Patty make better decisions after her mother's death. If the appraisal had been recommended in the course of a general estate plan, it might have been an easier step for Patty, not so directly connected to her mother's health and future plans. Some estate and financial planning professionals *may* suggest an evaluation of personal property, but, as we will see in the next chapter, collectible assets can routinely be overlooked and unspecified in basic estate plans.

Because personal property is not as *liquid* or as *readily valued* as other assets such as stocks and real estate, even when life changes are expected, the right choices are sometimes not made. Let's consider our examples:

Marvin, while making provisions for the asset that was most important to him personally, overlooked other items of value in his estate, and Jill felt she lacked the expertise to make a stronger case to Charles that the art collection should be valued separately from the other household contents.

Joe, while a knowledgeable collector, gave a gift to a family member who would appreciate it, but failed to provide Sarah with details about the possible worth of his library. Without John's help, she might have sold some of the collection quickly at a bargain price to someone who might have taken advantage of her lack of knowledge.

## WHAT THERE IS TO KNOW

When we set out to try to establish and maximize the value of a wide array of long-cherished family property, some basic questions we might ask are:

> Where can I sell some of my things?
> How do I find out what something is "worth"?
> How do I tell if something is old?
> When are appraisals necessary?
> When should an expert evaluate an item?
> What should I do with items that aren't collectible or valuable?

We are not going to be able to become overnight experts in the fields of antiques, appraisal, gemology, or the arcane history of a special type of memorabilia. But we *can* learn what questions to ask, where to get information, and how to begin to organize our collections so we can research and evaluate them.

## INVENTORY AND CATALOG

An appraiser, dealer, or other expert will want to see a list or inventory of your property in order to evaluate it. This can be as simple as making a list in a notebook. A digital camera is an important tool; you will definitely need one if you are going to sell on eBay or take advantage of the expertise of auction companies, many of whom will assess items for free if you email them a photograph. Appraisals done for insurance purposes today often require photographs as well; if you aren't computer savvy, get the expert in your family to show you how to use the camera. You can save photos on a CD, on your hard drive, or have prints made either at home or at the local drugstore.

If you have fragile paper materials such as stamps, comics, documents, or photographs, you can look for preservation sleeves, boxes, folders, and other supplies for storage from an **archival products dealer**. Database software for collection catalogs is also available from manufacturers such as *Liberty Street* and online at *Collectorz.Com*.

## STORAGE

If you have furniture or large quantities of items that you don't have room for, or if you are moving items from a distance, it may be best to put things in storage until you can make the best decisions about what to do with them. **Self-storage** is most convenient for items you may need to retrieve, but make sure you select a storage facility that has experience with antiques and other valuables. **Climate control** and **security, fire, and water protection** should be offered when you store valuable materials. Find out if your homeowner's insurance policy covers items in storage or if you need extra coverage. Don't wrap glass, porcelain, silver, or china objects directly in newspaper, which can cause staining, or bubble wrap, which can adhere to an object. You can purchase packing paper or tissue paper from a shipping supply company. EBay also sells shipping materials. Some professional packing and crating services also offer storage—for extremely rare, valuable, or fragile items—look on the web or in the phone book for **fine art shipping and crating services.**

## HELPERS

Who's the best web surfer in your family? Probably you also know a digital camera pro. Get family members involved to help you organize. Many of the suggestions I have for researching your collectibles utilize online resources, but, if you aren't computer savvy, there is always the phone book. If you aren't online yourself, and don't have anyone at home to help you, consider asking a local college if they have an **internship** program—an art history, design, literature, or other liberal arts major might be available to help you research your items or track down experts—maybe even for college credit. Check out your public and local university libraries as well—many libraries have **reference services** and can assist you with research projects. **Questia** is an online library with over six thousand research topics.

## CAN'T I JUST CALL SOMEONE?

Finding the right expert or the way to receive the best value for an antique or other heirloom is a process that can often involve more than one opinion. We will learn in this book where to look for information, how to find a qualified professional when we need one, and how to arrange for our collections and valuables to be sold for the best possible prices. Most of all, we will take a look at the most valuable and collectible types of property, how and where they've been selling, so we will know what to look for when trying to separate a rare treasure from an ordinary household object.

Whether you are evaluating collections as part of the estate planning process, as preparation for an upcoming move or "downsizing," or as the result of a death that has put you in an unexpected situation where it is necessary or advisable to determine the worth of valuables, many of the steps you will follow and tools you will use will be the same. As we know too well, life is full of unexpected turns. The *best* time to start an evaluation of potentially valuable items is *before* you get into a situation where there are more pressing demands on your time and emotions. This can create the groundwork for decisions in the future.

## 2

# Estate Planning Basics

When there is a death in the family, emotional and personal issues are in the forefront. It is hardly ever a good time to be wondering about what to do with collections or furniture. As in Patty's case, it can be a stressful time filled with overwhelming decisions. Some kinds of issues with personal property can be dealt with ahead of time as part of the **estate planning process**.

## WHAT IS ESTATE PLANNING?

The word "estate" refers to the assets and liabilities of a deceased person. The term can be used in two different ways—to refer to property owned by the decedent, as in "this Ming Dynasty vase is part of the Edward Wadsworth *estate*," but also to refer collectively to the heirs and persons administering the legal aspects of the property, as in "the *estate* of Edward Wadsworth plans to auction several important Ming vases."

"Estate planning" refers to all the aspects of the distribution of a person's assets to those who are legally entitled to receive them. Financial advisors also use the term to refer to the tax and legal aspects of the estate—the drawing up of documents such as wills and trusts, and the management of financial assets to deal with various aspects of estate taxation. Estates are taxed at the federal level, but the administration of estates is regulated by the state in which an individual resides.

## WILLS

The planning process begins when a person is still alive, when a **will** or a **trust** is created. A will is a relatively simple document. Most of us are familiar to some degree with the terminology—a person states in writing how he wishes to disperse his property, or make other provisions, upon his death. Wills are typically drawn up by attorneys, but in most states a will does not have to be executed by a lawyer to be a legal document. It must, however, meet certain conditions, such as the fact that it must be witnessed, usually by two individuals, and in most cases an executor or administrator must be appointed. Various states allow certain types of "streamlined" wills, such as preprinted "statutory" wills or handwritten "holographic" wills that are not witnessed.

Whether or not it is required, it is a good idea to have legal advice when drawing up a will. Estates can be challenged, and a claim against an estate can tie up the process of distributing property. Existing wills can be changed or modified, either by adding a **codicil** to an existing will or by drawing up a new one. Changes to wills are generally made if life circumstances of an individual change with respect to marriage, having children, a change in financial situation, or the decision to make a specific gift or bequest.

In a will, an **executor** or personal representative is designated to handle the affairs of the estate. That individual will apply for an appointment from the court in the jurisdiction where the estate is to be processed. A judge will review the will and the certificate of death, and grant the executor legal authority to manage the property and business of the decedent. This process is the "opening act" in the procedure known as **probate.**

In probate, the court must supervise the activities of the executor and approve his distribution of the assets of the estate. If there are claims or liabilities, these must be legally satisfied before property can be given to the heirs. Most of the time, an attorney will help the executor manage the probate, submitting the required documents to the court and advising the executor on the steps in the process.

## TRUSTS

There are many kinds of **trusts**, some established while individuals are still alive and administering their own affairs, and some established by a will, to provide for the future ownership and management of the estate. Trusts serve many different purposes but the most common, especially for people with smaller and simpler estates, is to **bypass the process of probate**.

A trust is a legal entity that takes ownership of property. The assets are then administered by a trustee. A trustee can be an individual, which is common with simple family trusts, or a professional entity such as a bank. Let's say you are John Jones and your attorney draws up a personal trust for you. The name of the trust may be something like "The John Jones Living Trust, dated January 1, 2005," and the trustees may be John and Mary Jones. Property belonging to John and Mary, for instance their home, securities brokerage accounts, and bank accounts, must now be **registered in the name of their trust** to be considered part of the trust's assets. To do this you need to notify your banks, securities brokers, and title companies that you have established a trust, and usually provide them with a copy of it.

A trust spells out the future "chain of command" in terms of inheritances and administration of the trust's property. The "successor trustee" is someone who assumes control of the trust when the existing trustee dies or becomes incapacitated.

Trusts have few disadvantages. The federal tax rate for a trust is generally higher than for an individual. A trust may have to be amended when there are changes in family circumstances or new estate tax laws.

## ESTATE PLANNING PROS

Everyone should have some kind of estate plan, no matter how simple. An attorney specializing in family law, probate, and estates can help you draft a plan and decide if a will or trust is best for you. In the estate planning process, you may also utilize the help of a tax advisor, financial planner, stockbroker, life insurance agent, and realtor. The ownership status of your financial accounts, real estate, life insurance policies, and bank accounts should be reviewed to make sure they are in accordance with your plan. Older wills and trusts should be reevaluated regularly in light of ongoing changes in estate tax laws.

## PERSONAL PROPERTY IN ESTATES

Tangible personal property—furniture, jewelry, antiques, fine art, collections, and other similar assets—is property that is **not as readily or easily valued** as financial instruments or real estate. There is no "registered" or regulated ownership of this kind of property. Some states have taxes on property associated with businesses, and there are statutes about certain types of personal property as it concerns real estate. Basically though, most personal property is considered to be household goods and personal effects, and is included in an individual's estate.

As part of the probate process, or the management of an estate by a trustee, an **inventory and appraisal** of the estate will be conducted. Depending on the size and complexity of the estate, this process can be simple or detailed. Household objects may be lumped together and their value estimated in a general way. This method is often used when there is an uncomplicated family situation and personal property is being passed to a surviving spouse and children, especially when the estate is small enough not to require a federal tax return.

In larger estates where there are known to be valuable collections, or where disposition of personal property assets must be made in exactly equal shares, the trustee or probate referee will usually require a more formal appraisal (see chapter 3).

One common problem or mistake that is frequently made with personal property is **not being specific enough** about its disposition in the estate planning documents. Often a will or trust will simply state that the personal property of the decedent is to be divided equally among the heirs and beneficiaries named. In the turbulent environment of a time of family sadness, unpredictable situations and emotions can arise.

Caroline and her sister, Trish, had a bitter dispute over their mother's diamond ring after her death. She had many other pieces of jewelry, but her will had made no mention of it specifically, simply stating that her personal possessions should be divided between her two daughters.

Caroline's husband asked their lawyer to come up with a solution, but to no avail. The attorney even proposed separating the diamond from its setting, and creating two rings, one with the original setting and one with the diamond, but the sisters still could not agree. Caroline was surprised at the degree of emnity brought on by the situation. She and Trish were both upset over losing their mother, but feelings of anger and mistrust toward her sister were something she had not expected to experience.

Eventually the attorney for the estate contacted a gemologist-appraiser to evaluate the ring and a number of other pieces. Despite its sentimental appeal, the diamond ring turned out to be considerably less valuable than two other rings, a star sapphire and a light blue Ceylon sapphire.

"It made sense, later on," Caroline remembers. "The diamond was Mother's engagement ring. In later years Dad could afford to buy her better jewelry. But we always recalled her wearing the diamond, especially as children. She would let us try it on and tell the story of how surprised she had been to receive it. It was a tangible memory of her. It became a symbol of how difficult it was for us to let her go."

Eventually the sisters agreed to a coin toss for the ring. Caroline won the toss, but when she saw the disappointment on her sister's face, she agreed that Trish could have it. "Suddenly the whole thing had more perspective. Mother will always be with us, no matter who has the diamond. But if we had gone over the jewelry and discussed things ahead of time, we might have avoided some hurtful moments. It just never occurred to us. I guess most people don't think of doing this. It's so much easier to avoid the whole subject."

Financial and legal advisors recommend today that collections and other valuables be itemized *specifically* in estate documents, with direct instructions about their disposition.

Other problems can arise when potentially important property has not been identified.

Todd was executor of his father's estate. He had no idea that the three old landscape paintings that had hung on the wall of his father's study were valuable examples of the nineteenth-century American Hudson River School, two by important artists of the movement, Thomas Cole and Thomas Doughty.

"They were just pictures to me. They had been in the house ever since I was a child, and I couldn't remember ever discussing them with my father. We only learned they were potentially valuable when an antique dealer came over to look at some of the furniture. It just happened he was familiar with the style, and commented what lovely examples they were. It got me thinking about them, and I did some research. Eventually the paintings appraised at over $100,000 for the three. I would have probably never thought of looking into it."

My friend Kim told me a story of her elderly Aunt Rosalyn, who was found one day writing on little labels and sticking them on the undersides of several pieces of antique china.

"None of us could figure out what she was doing! We thought maybe that she was senile. It turns out she was writing the names of the china patterns and the makers on the labels. She wanted to make sure her heirs knew what the pieces were, and wouldn't just discard them."

## PLANNING AHEAD

Aunt Rosalyn's method might seem eccentric, but the idea behind it is a good one. Many financial planners recommend **an inventory of assets** as a tool in helping to make decisions of many different types, not just those regarding estates. Inventories of collections, information such as receipts or descriptions of property, appraisals done for insurance purposes, even notes jotted down about the origin or identity of antiques, art, and other belongings can be stored with estate planning documents to be used when the estate is being valued.

Life can be unpredictable, and decisions about property often need to be made for other reasons besides a death in the family—a move, an illness, or other change of life circumstances. Taking the time to identify and value property and collections before a death can have many benefits. Not only will the estate process run more smoothly, but you can also uncover assets and potential important sources of liquidity.

One important thing we will learn about the valuation of antiques, art, and other collectibles is that **information** about their origin can be vital.

An important step you can take in preserving the value of family treasures is to find out as much as you can about when and where they were acquired, and how long they have been in the family.

Small details about the history and identity of items can **greatly increase their value**. Often the knowledge of facts and history of many family heirlooms is lost with the passage of time, with the information goes the chance to authenticate a potentially valuable item.

# 3

# VALUE AND APPRAISALS

## WHAT'S IT WORTH?

One of the first things we might wish to know about an antique, piece of art, or other collectible is its approximate value. But . . . what is actually meant by "value"? Possibly more confounding, what *creates* value in a collectible asset? These two questions have been making the world of collecting go round for the last several centuries.

In the stock market, value is an up-to-the-minute quote that can be instantly read on a screen. There is no mystery as to what a share of IBM is currently "worth." Stocks traded on public exchanges are continuously valued as they change hands, and have a stated closing price at the end of every trading day. You can easily punch up a quote on any financial website, or check the stock tables in any major newspaper.

With real estate, there are usually plentiful records of **comparable sales** to examine. Factors such as prices per square foot in a geographic area, or rates such as income capitalization are also used in real estate valuation. Where there are not a large number of comparable sales to consider, sometimes replacement costs are used.

## WHY ARE COLLECTIBLES DIFFERENT?

With art objects and collectibles, the situation is somewhat different. Often we have a one-of-a-kind item, or an item that was made only in limited quantity. Many objects have been hand-crafted or have other attributes of rarity. Some seemingly baffling contradictions come up when researching values:

- A large diamond ring may be worth considerably less than a smaller one.
- A book from 1969 might be worth much more than one from 1850.
- A modern chrome chair might sell for a higher price than an eighteenth-century antique chair.
- A small gold coin may be worth thousands of times its weight in gold bullion.

How can we possibly gain an understanding of why some things are valuable and some are not?

## WHAT CREATES VALUE?

The Holy Grail, or maybe the sixty-four-thousand-dollar question of collecting is: What causes an antique, a piece of art, a rare gem, or a collectible, to be valuable and sought after?

Dealers, scholars, connoisseurs, and other old hands spend lifetimes examining and studying objects, yet there is no such thing as an "encyclopedia of values" to tell us exactly how much things are supposed to be worth.

In a very general sense, value for collectibles is related to prices at auctions and in retail situations for similar items. But there are often not many sales of items that are *exactly* the same!

So, what else is used to determine value? A few basic principles apply across a fairly wide spectrum of collectibles:

## Condition

With few exceptions, the most valuable items are in the best condition. Terms like "mint" and "flawless" reflect the top of the condition scale. The better the condition, usually the greater the value.

## Scarcity

Rare or hard-to-find items, or items originally produced in a small quantity, are more valuable than those which are in plentiful supply. Sometimes a *mistake*, such as a misprint in a book, an error in printing a stamp or striking a coin, was corrected after only a few imperfect examples escaped into public hands, creating a sought-after oddity.

## Provenance

This word sounds French, but the French word for it is actually *origine*. This should give you a clue to its meaning. The dictionary defines "**provenance**" as "**time and place of origin**." With collectibles, it can mean any kind of documentation, of origin, and also history of ownership.

Elements of provenance include: having been part of a particular collection or exhibition, an original sales receipt, a news article, a photograph, any identifying material or proof of previous ownership. A piece that is signed or stamped by an artist or manufacturer, because it is easier to verify, is *most* often more valuable than a similar unsigned piece.

## Quality

One of the more elusive elements to define simply!

Typically a high degree of craftsmanship, the quality of intrinsic materials, especially with gemstones, and excellent artistic or design attributes, all contribute to value. Where a piece is from a particular period or style, the **execution** of the design and the **reflection of the style** through the design can enhance value. Sometimes, though, a design that is more unusual for its period will stand out.

## Popularity

Collectible assets, including the works of artists, the writings of authors, styles of dress, furniture, interior design, and decorative arts, are forever going in and out of vogue. "Hot" toys and games have been the subjects of fads for generations. Simply put, if people want something and consider it appealing, the price can go up.

Psychologists and sociologists have studied cultural fashion—including why certain dog breeds become desirable—without reaching many conclusions as to why things go in and out of favor.

No matter what they may find, the popularity of styles, or periods of art and design, has been an important factor in the world of collecting for many centuries. Today, furniture and decorative objects from the Arts and Crafts and Modern era are enjoying a huge boom—a couple of decades ago, these might have easily been picked up in thrift stores. Desirability is an important—and unpredictable—factor in determining value, and one that is also likely to be in flux!

## MARKETS AND THE MARKETPLACE

Another element in determining value for a collectible is the **marketplace** itself. This is different from the way stocks and real estate work. The business of selling stocks and real estate is regulated, and transactions occur in a fairly limited set of circumstances. Sales of "like" items in securities and real estate tend to occur in "like" situations, and result in comparable prices.

Antiques and other collectible assets are sold in a *wide variety of venues*—in exclusive shops, at antique malls, at auction in major world capitals and in smaller cities and towns, between private parties, at flea markets, at garage sales, and, now more than ever before, online.

Because there is a wide range of settings in which the sale can take place, the market *and* the parties involved can have an impact on price. The selling price of an object can be directly related to how well the seller is able to attract a buyer. Sometimes important collectors are buying, other times they are absent from the market. Sometimes an item will sell for a higher price at a "major" auction, because of its visibility and the caliber of the collectors who will be bidding.

This is why, when you review records of selling prices for many objects that *sound* similar, there can be a considerable variance in results. The works of a particular artist may sell better in England than in Chicago. A piece that belonged to a celebrity—such as some of the household items that sold in Sotheby's February 2005 auction of property from John F. Kennedy's homes—may sell for many thousands more than a very similar item that comes from an ordinary estate. Some pieces may sell for higher prices when placed in an auction with other important or notable objects.

Professional dealers and auction companies have a sense of the value of items they evaluate, but even they can be amazed or surprised when certain pieces skyrocket above their estimates, or fail to bring a reserve bid. Their success in marketing valuable items comes partly from placing an item in an appropriate venue where it will attract the right type of buyer or investor.

## GRADING AND AUTHENTICATION

**Grading** is a new twist on a relatively old concept that has revolutionized the market for some collectibles. To some extent, it has been helping to improve some variables in pricing.

Grading means an **evaluation of the condition** of an item. It can be said that collectibles have always been informally graded by their sellers, since any description includes some facts about condition.

The new type of **third-party grading** refers to an outside evaluation by a grading specialist, someone who is **uninvolved in the buying or selling of the item**.

## GRADING HISTORY

Third-party grading was first developed in the rare coin collecting world in the 1980s. Because the condition of a rare coin has such a drastic influence on its value, it was thought that dealers involved in purchasing and selling of coins were not always objective about the grades they assigned.

Coins had been informally graded since around the early 1900s. In 1948 a well-known numismatist named Dr. William Sheldon first attempted to standardize coin grading with a scale that ran from 1 at the lowest to 70 at the highest. Although many collectors agreed with the scale, there was not always agreement on standards of interpretation. When dealers issued grades on coins they intended to resell, it created an obvious conflict of interest.

By 1985 the coin industry agreed that a new system was needed to protect investors and enhance the integrity of the marketplace. The first third-party grading company for coins, *Professional Coin Grading Service*, known as *PCGS*, evolved in Newport Beach, California. Several major competitors soon followed. Since 1986, PCGS has graded over 10 million coins, with an estimated value of over 16 billion dollars.

Once a coin has been given a grade it is generally sealed in a tamper-resistant capsule along with its grading certificate. The coin can be said to have **more liquidity** in this state, since once it has been officially graded and sealed, more investors will have confidence in buying it without having to examine it in person.

Third-party grading has expanded to more collectibles, notably comics, toys, baseball cards, stamps, and autographed memorabilia. With the tremendous rise of internet trading in a universe of collectible items, grading has transformed the marketplace and impacted values significantly. The grading process itself is not the same as an **estimate** of value, but it can greatly **enhance** value.

## WHAT IS AN APPRAISAL?

An "**appraisal**" is a professional assessment of the value of a piece of property.

Appraisals are used in all types of property, including real estate, aircraft, livestock, machinery, and factory and farm equipment. An appraiser who deals with art, antiques, and other collectibles is usually referred to as a **personal property appraiser**. He or she may have a speciality in fine art or in antiques, or may be a specialist in generalized household contents. Usually an appraiser will have a separate certification in **jewelry**.

Appraisers are trained and certified by professional organizations, the largest of which is the American Society of Appraisers (ASA), founded in 1936 and incorporated in 1952. The ASA has over five thousand members, and has some of the more stringent membership requirements. To become an ASA certified personal property appraiser, a candidate must pass through a series of educational, professional, and experience requirements and pass a series of exams.

Personal property appraisers are not required to be licensed by states in the same manner as real estate appraisers, but they are generally expected to adhere to the professional standards of the appraisal industry. In 1989, as part of the federal bailout of the savings and loan industry, the Uniform Standards of Professional Appraisal Practice, known as USPAP, was mandated. Most appraisers trained today receive education in the standards, guidelines and ethics of USPAP.

## TWO KINDS OF APPRAISALS

In the world of personal property, there are two different kinds of appraisals: **replacement cost** and **fair market value**.

### Replacement Cost

The **replacement cost** appraisal is typically used for insurance purposes. Replacement cost can be similar to a retail price or the cost of re-creating something. In the case of a rare or valuable item, or a collection that has importance because of its size and scope, replacement costs can be difficult to estimate. Sometimes replacement cost may have a relationship to the original cost or purchase price of an item, but not always, especially when a piece of art or an antique has appreciated.

### Fair Market Value

The **fair market value** appraisal is used in estate situations where property needs to be divided fairly among heirs. It can also be used to determine the value of an item that is going to be donated to charity (more about donations in chapter 17).

The IRS defines "fair market value" as *the price that an item might sell for in the open market, in a sale between a willing buyer and a willing seller, both with knowledge of "the relevant facts."* The appraiser's job in a fair market value appraisal is to determine that price through research and knowledge of both the item and the marketplace. There are times when fair market value might be similar to the retail price of an item. This is where the expertise and resources available to the appraiser come into play.

There is a third type of valuation, which might be considered **liquidation** value, or as some refer to it, **marketable cash value**. This is the "low end" of the value scale, the prices things might sell for at a garage sale or if they are otherwise quickly disposed of.

It is important to talk with your appraiser and ask a number of questions. Find out his or her background and qualifications. Don't be afraid to ask what information resources he will be using to make his evaluations. Make sure you both are clear about the purpose of the appraisal.

The fees for an appraisal vary by the size and complexity of the item or collection. An appraiser may charge by the hour, anywhere from $75 to $400. He may be able to give you a quote for the completed appraisal upon seeing the property and estimating the amount of time the work will take.

The finished appraisal should be in writing, with details of the items. In some cases the appraiser will provide sources for the replacement or market values.

## WHEN SHOULD I GET AN APPRAISAL?

Appraisal of personal property is not an exact science. You might get appraisals that differ from one another for the same object, depending on the appraiser's knowledge of the particular asset. The ASA offers personal property certification for over twenty different subspecialities of antiques and art—firearms, Oriental rugs, clocks, silver and metalware, and books among them—but there still could be an object or area difficult to research, or where prices have been fluctuating.

Generally an appraisal is recommended:

- when you are dividing an estate or planning to do so and want to insure that heirs receive equal portions;
- when you wish to donate property and are eligible to receive a fair market value deduction; or
- when you want to insure your valuables.

If you are just trying to "get an idea" what your collection or a specific item is worth, an appraisal can be costly, and it is **not** a guarantee that your items will sell for the appraised value.

## CAN MY APPRAISER HELP ME SELL AN ITEM?

The ethical appraiser should **never offer to purchase an item directly from you**. They should also never charge you a fee based on a percentage of an item's value—this would constitute an obvious conflict of interest. They should not suggest to you that you trade them any item in lieu of a fee, and they should disclose to you if they are working on behalf of any other client in any capacity.

It is common, however, for an appraiser also to work as a dealer, or sometimes a broker who can help negotiate sales between clients and dealers. They may even make referrals to auction houses and receive a finder's fee for placing an item in a sale. It is perfectly legitimate for an appraiser to give you referrals to someone who may be interested in purchasing your item or marketing it to their own clientele. However, you **don't need** a referral from an appraiser to deal with an auction company. Auction companies of all sizes welcome inquiries from anyone who has a possible item for them to sell, so don't be intimidated. You can read more about auctions in chapter 15.

## DOES MY APPRAISAL MEAN IT'S AUTHENTIC?

Appraisers are not always qualified to evaluate the **authenticity** of an item. They may have varying degrees of expertise in some areas. A jewelry appraiser may be a certified gemologist with a laboratory. An art appraiser may have a speciality in a specific artist or school. But not every appraiser can authenticate every kind of antique or fine art item beyond a reasonable doubt.

A good appraiser will give you advice about which of your items need further evaluation in order to arrive at a probable worth that will be as accurate as possible. If necessary, he will suggest that the piece be evaluated by an **expert**, a specialist who may not be involved with the marketplace of the item, but who may have knowledge of the history and special qualities of a specific category of antique or art object. Many appraisers will have a "rolodex" of contacts they can suggest you call on for this purpose, but you may also look for one on your own to get a second or a third opinion on a potentially valuable item.

## THE ROLE OF THE EXPERT

Who is an expert—and what can we expect to learn from one?

An expert is someone who has spent his or her life dealing extensively with a specific type of antique object or area of fine art. The expert may be a dealer, a curator, an academic, a scholar, or a researcher who has authored catalogs and written books about the history of his or her subject area. The expert may possibly be an experienced collector, someone with a passion for a certain period, genre, or designer. An expert may be on the staff of a major auction house, or if not, the specialists there may know where to find one. In a foreign country, the expert may be a member of a government cultural ministry, or a historian or archivist designated by government officials as an authority. Students and protégés will spend time with an expert in order to learn from him or her. The expert may be renowned, or may be someone local who has just spent his or her life and work on a specific subject.

## WHAT THE EXPERT KNOWS

The expert should be able to assist in determining the age, origin, authenticity, period, manufacturer, designer, materials, and other attributes of a piece. An expert can give a professional opinion as to its identity, but not necessarily as to its market value. Staff experts at museums, for instance, are generally prohibited by museum policies from making estimates of valuations. Appraisers, auction companies, and dealers will use the information the expert provides in helping to value and sell a piece.

How does the expert know what he knows? Years of study, observing, handling, researching, and maybe something of a "sixth sense." The expert is attuned to materials, wear, signs of aging, and subtle elements of design and craftsmanship, and will know when different styles and techniques were used when, and in many cases, what items have been widely reproduced.

## Where to Look for an Expert

- major and regional auction companies
- historical societies and museums
- university art and history departments
- collector clubs and associations
- referrals from authors and journalists who have written about art, antiques, and historical periods
- some dealers are experts and may give you referrals to others

## When Should I Have an Expert Evaluation?

- to assist with an identification or an appraisal by verifying age, materials, style, probable origin, or other facts
- if you have an item you suspect is valuable but does not have a signature or other identifying marks
- if your item is known to be valuable and the expert's opinion will **add to the provenance**
- if your item appears to be high quality but lacks a provenance or history
- if you have a type of item that has been known to have been reproduced or copied

## IS IT REAL OR FAKE?

Fakes, forgeries, and reproductions of all kinds have existed in the art and decorative arts world for centuries. There have been some very famous examples of works owned by museums that were later found to be modern reproductions. During the Old Master era, paintings were routinely copied by young artists as part of their training, and as a way to study and record art development. After all, there was no photography at the time!

Often reproductions were made because the original item was popular, and people down through the centuries wanted to own something just like it. Successful books have been reprinted; desirable furniture styles, glassware, lamps, china, and other antique items have been copied; paintings have been turned into prints and posters, prints and posters themselves into later generations of prints and posters.

Art and antique experts can usually tell a newer reproduction of an antique item by slight differences in lines, materials, and other details.

## FAKE OR REPRODUCTION?

There is a difference between a reproduction made in the style of a popular antique, and an outright forgery, made to be passed off as a valuable item.

Tiffany Lamps, art nouveau glass, Arts and Crafts pottery, scrimshaw, belt buckles, collectible kitchen items such as cookie jars, autographed photos, paintings and graphic works of famous artists—these are only some of the items that have been forged and faked on purpose. There is a middle ground of items too: inexpensive imports, not meant to pass off as antiques, but still occasionally finding their way to dealers' shelves with high price tags.

There are a number of guidebooks on the market about how to identify fakes and reproductions, particularly of glass, pottery, and other small items. Remember, though, if you are inexperienced in dealing with antiques, your eye is not trained to recognize some of the differences in markings and quality of production noted in these guides.

Even dealers with a wealth of experience have been occasionally fooled by fakes. Remember this is part of the territory with certain types of antiques. Some fake items are more difficult to detect than others. If you encounter one among your valuables, don't be disheartened, especially if you don't know the complete history of the piece. It may have been acquired reasonably or sold innocently. In any case, the more knowledge you acquire about your own items will help you learn the right questions to ask to protect yourself from possible fakes of the future!

# 4

# INFORMATION...
# PLEASE!

D oes this sound like you? You have furniture, silver, jewelry, paintings, or books that have been in the family for some time. You've got a desk full of old papers and some boxes of old clothes packed away. In the garage are piles of magazines, in the dining room are cabinets of china and curios.

You might have some unusual items here and there. Some old scientific instruments or World War II souvenirs. A collection of pens or knives. Boxes of antique sewing patterns, thimbles, and fabric swatches. You find some coins in packages, some old sheet music.

On the wall are old-looking prints in frames. Quilts in the blanket chest, gold-framed mirrors in the bedroom, several jewelry boxes brimming with beads and pins. You find a box of old metal toy soldiers in the closet. A Chinese-looking vase with gold trim has been on the mantle for years.

You decide it's time to find out more about your treasures. What are they? How old are they? Are any of them valuable, or should they be given away? Where can you sell them?

Most important, how are you going to find answers to these questions?

## WHO CAN HELP?

If you found a box of stock certificates or a pile of mutual fund and bank statements, you would call a stockbroker. If you find deeds and legal documents pertaining to rental properties or other real estate investments, you might call a realtor, or ask your attorney to help you research the titles and ownership status of the properties.

With personal property, there might not be *one specific person* you can turn to who knows all there is to know about everything under the sun. Extensive knowledge about art, different types of antiques, books, jewelry, and collectibles might not all reside with one person! In fact, there are many experts on every subject who know little outside their areas of expertise.

So, how are you going to find the right expert, or the right place to sell something that you might have? This is a complicated question. You could start looking in the phone book for appraisers and antique dealers, or stop by bookstores and art galleries, trying to get answers, but the first thing you are possibly going to be asked when you call someone and say you have an item is—**what is it?**

If you aren't sure, you won't be able to get far.

Additionally, the first dealer or appraiser you might contact may not have **expertise** in the area of the item you want to sell or evaluate. If you call a local auction company to help you sell the contents of a household, certain valuable or salable items might be overlooked, or the evaluator may not be aware of their value, and they may be swept up by a dealer or collector who knows what he is buying.

## TAKING INVENTORY

As we mentioned in chapter 1, when you get ready to research your collections, the first step is to take inventory. You can start by making a general list by category, and describing the items to the best of your abilities, just as they appear to you. When you have your rudimentary list, you can go on to try to identify and describe your items further.

## WHAT THERE IS TO KNOW

A description of an antique or fine art item for sale will include several elements:

> What kind of piece is it? What materials is it made from?
> What are the size and dimensions of the piece?
> What is the approximate age of the piece, and/or what period or style does it belong to?
> Who designed or manufactured the piece?
> Where was it originally sold, if known?

## SO, WHAT IS IT?

Let's take a look at that first list you made, a simple inventory of items that you created.

We might see some listings that sound like this:

> antique blue and white plate
> diamond and pearl stick pin
> Hummel Figurine—Boy Playing Flute
> old Winnie the Pooh children's book

In order to more accurately determine if these items have value, more details are needed.

A more complete identification may sound something like this:

> 10-inch Flow Blue Dinner Plate, Kenworth, Johnson Brothers, c. 1900
> pin, diamond and seed pearl, designed as baton, 18K gold mount, 1 1/2-inch bead-set with 59 old mine-cut diamonds, seed pearl accents
> Hummel—"Serenade"—#85/II, 7 1/2 inches—Trademark 3
> *The House at Pooh Corner*, A. A. Milne, E. P. Dutton, 34th printing, September 1928. Pink boards, gilt title, decorated endpapers

You might be thinking now—How could I do this? Where does this information come from? Surprisingly, these types of identifications are not difficult to make. You just need to know where to look for the information that will help you.

## WHY IDENTIFY?

The more complete an identification of an item you can make, the better. It will be easier for you to work with a dealer, or someone you may hire to hold an estate sale, or to get better prices selling on your own. You won't necessarily get to the point of making distinctions between subtle differences in design, obscure signatures on antique paintings, or fine points of editions of very rare books. What you can hope to achieve is to gather enough **descriptive details** about your items and their possible age to get a more accurate sense of their *possible* value.

Some items are easier to identify than others. The three examples listed above are particularly easy ones. The Johnson Brothers dinnerware patterns and Hummel figurines have been extensively catalogued, with photographs. Unlike thousands of other rare books, every one of the many Winnie the Pooh reprints is dated with the printing edition noted.

Other antiques, particularly furniture, are harder to identify accurately. An expert at a major auction company told me the story of an antique sofa. The piece could have been made in either England or America in the very early 1800s. The furniture experts at the auction house felt the sofa would have more value if it could be identified as early American. But even the furniture experts with their knowledge were not sure of the sofa's origin. Eventually, a small chunk of secondary wood from the sofa's frame was analyzed by the forestry department at a midwestern university. The frame contained sycamore and gum wood, not available in England!

You may not be able to do quite this kind of detective work on your own antiques. But you can come up with a working description, a set of facts that should include:

- the function or name of the piece
- the materials, size, dimensions, colors, images portrayed
- any identifying marks, signatures, labels, inscriptions, or evidence of ownership

- the style and the approximate or estimated age, and, perhaps most important, *any factual knowledge you have about its history*

The word "factual" is significant here. There are old stories—not all of them accurate—that abound in every family about the history of heirlooms. If your information is only anecdotal, make note of this in your description. Today more than ever before, information we can use for our descriptions and identifications is close to our fingertips.

## REFERENCE BOOKS

Countless books about antiques and collectibles provide help in identifying many different kinds of items. A reference book may be titled something like *The Complete Guide to Furniture Styles* (Louise Ade Boger, Waveland Press, 1997) or *Victorian Glass: Specialties of the 19th Century* (Ruth Webb Lee, Tuttle, 1985). It will not have prices or market trends, but will detail history, design, styles, important artists, and manufacturers of items like the ones you have.

Reference books can be found at public libraries, college libraries, used bookstores, antique malls, in museum archives, in the libraries of dealers and collectors, and through book websites like *Amazon* and *ABE* (*Advanced Book Exchange*). Many smaller online book dealers such as *JR's Collector Reference Books, Inc.* and *Robby's Bookshelf* also specialize in antique and collectible reference.

**Library websites** are a good place to search for reference resources. You can try a site like the *New York Public Library*, which has extensive titles listed under its **Research Libraries—Art and Architecture Collection.** Library sites are huge and can be complex to navigate—the NYPL has both live chat and email help.

## PRICE GUIDES

A price guide is a kind of catalog that will list recent values and selling prices. They are often called **Value and Identification Guides**, since you can use them to identify objects by comparison to descriptions of the priced items listed there.

Price guides are researched, written, and compiled by antique or collectible specialists, using records of sales from dealers, auction companies, shows, and sometimes lately from online venues. The price guide authors look for up-to-date information available from the most reliable sources. They cover shows and auctions, correspond with dealers, and try to find out everything they can that is going on in their marketplace.

Many guides are general, with multiple categories from furniture to porcelain and glass. Some are specific to a certain type of collectible, even a certain manufacturer. When condition is not noted, an item in a price guide should be assumed to be in mint or fine condition.

Price guides may list items **alphabetically, by manufacturer, or by style.** In an antique furniture price guide, for instance, you may see categories such as Chair and Sideboard, but also Heppelwhite, Queen Anne, or American Golden Oak. In a glass price guide, glass may be categorized by its color, such as Cranberry Glass, its style or period, such as Depression Glass, or its manufacturer or designer, such as Lalique.

Prices of collectibles may fluctuate continually. In some guides, prices are reported in ranges. A good price guide will usually contain a short overview of what has been going on in its particular market, or if it covers many subject areas, a synopsis of trends in each. It may go into detail as to where some of the sales have taken place, or list the general pricing sources.

If you have a whole houseful of items and don't know where to start, begin with a general guide, such as *Kovel's Antiques and Collectibles Price List*, to get a feeling of how things are organized. Price guides can range from general to very specific for a certain period, manufacturer, or type of item.

Sam had collected Hot Wheels model cars since the 1970s and asked me how he could find out what they were worth. He brought a few of the cars over so we could look them up together. All of the cars had dates stamped on their undersides, so we could date them without difficulty. **Karen O'Brien**'s *12th Edition Toys and Prices—2005* guide had Hot Wheels cars broken down by model years and series. We could tell from the guide that only a very few cars from 1997 and 1998 (Mint in Package) were attracting prices of more than a few dollars. Two cars in his group with metal bottoms, both stamped 1974, however, seemed to warrant further investigation, as some of the 1970s models in the price guide had higher prices.

At this point, Sam needed to look for a more specific Hot Wheels price guide, to help him identify and further research the prices of the cars he had in his collection that might be more valuable.

## WHERE TO FIND PRICE GUIDES

Price guides are sometimes available for browsing in antique malls, at shops and shows, at libraries, in used book stores, and increasingly in online formats. There are also **weekly and monthly price guide magazines** that are issued for coins, stamps, and some other popular collectibles such as toys. Many dealers sell guides—one doll shop I visited had over a hundred guides for sale.

Remember that prices you see in a guide are meant to serve only as a *guide*. It means that an object has sold once for that price. Your item may be similar but not identical to the one in the guide. The price might represent a trend in the market that has since changed. A variety of factors can exist that might make the value of your item different from one in a guide. Consider a guide as a starting point. It can educate you as to the market for your type of asset.

## INTERNET RESOURCES

A huge and growing wealth of online resources exist for collectors, and all of it is just a few clicks away. By the time this book is published, the sites I have listed in the Internet Resource Guide may have grown or changed, and many more new ones will be available.

But if you know *how* to search for information about your collectibles, you will find many helpful sites, probably some that had not come into being while I wrote this, where you can research everything from porcelain marks to comics to fine art to silver patterns.

*What You Can Find Online*
photographs and descriptions of antiques and other valuable objects
identification of different periods and styles
questions and answers from professionals and other collectors
directories of marks and hallmarks

asking prices at retailers and galleries

auction results from all over the world, and on eBay

price guides and reference books to purchase

Where will you find all this? Here are a few places to start looking:

## DISCUSSION BOARDS, NEWSGROUPS, AND FORUMS

Many collectibles websites have **discussion forums and bulletin boards** where you can ask questions about your items. *EBay*'s forums are possibly the largest and most extensive of these but there are many other websites such as *WorldCollectors.net*, and *Collect.com* (Krause Publications' Resource site) where you can find opportunities to ask questions.

*Individual collector clubs* and many dealer websites also have information boards and answer questions by email.

Browse these forums first to get an idea to see what kinds of questions have been previously asked and answered. On eBay many participants in the forums will provide identification of themselves and their qualifications. They may be professionals, or they may just be knowledgeable collectors who enjoy the fun and learning involved with helping others. Often you can post or email a photo and get a free opinion, particularly on the identification of an item.

*Newsgroups* on collectibles can be found all over the internet. Several of the oldest and most frequented are from *Usenet*. You can find a menu at Usenet's main web address (www.usenet.com/).

The newsgroups associated with collectibles are in the "rec" (for recreation or hobby) category such as rec.antiques or rec.models.railroad. *Rec.collecting* has quite a few subgroups such as cards, dolls, coins and stamps, with more subcategories under cards and other sports memorabilia.

Collectibles newsgroups also can be found on *AOL*, *Yahoo*, and *Google*.

Newsgroups and forum members often steer clear of "valuation" or appraisal questions, and focus instead on identification, marks, history, manufacturer information, and little known details or tricks of the trade. People who frequent internet forums are there generally because they have enthusiasm and knowledge, and love an opportunity to interact. They can point you in the right direction, provide you with valuable tips, and refer you to other resources.

## COMPLETED AUCTION RESULTS

When you get an idea what kind of collectible you have, you can access **completed auction results** at the websites of many auction houses. Spend time on the auction websites researching their calendars and getting to know how the site is organized.

Some of the larger auction companies with easy-to-find results include *Sotheby's*, *Christie's*, *Swann Galleries*, *Doyle New York*, and *Bonham's*.

Websites such as *ArtNet* and *ArtFact* are in the process of collating thousands of fine art auction results.

The *Americana Exchange* tracks rare book auctions.

Stamp results can be found on an increasing number of sites such as *StampAuction.Com*. Many of these sites require registration and/or subscription, but more free sites are also coming along.

**Completed results on eBay** are available for thirty days after an item sells, and only to registered users. More about eBay in chapter 15, but until then, it is well worth becoming an eBay member long before you plan to sell anything, just so you can begin to review completed items. You can find completed items by using the search function to select a category, and then clicking "**Completed listings**" under "Search Options" in the yellow column on the left of the screen.

You can view the original listing this way, including the bidding history and final selling price. It is a good way of reviewing a description of an item. If bidders have asked questions of the seller about the item, sometimes they will be posted as part of the listing.

## MAGAZINES AND NEWSLETTERS

As fast as the internet is growing, antiques and collectibles periodicals are keeping pace with it. A number of informative **online magazines** are available where you can read about auctions and get access to identification resources.

*The Maine Antiques Digest* has a showcase of gallery advertisers who feature items you can browse. They maintain an auction calendar, a database of auction results, a library of American furniture makers, reviews of hundreds of reference books, and dealer directories.

*Art and Antiques* has an identification and appraisal query page, discussion forums, art gallery search, news, and links to appraisers and dealers.

*Diamond Galleries*, a dealer in comics, posters, Disney articles, and toys, has a free newsletter called *Scoop*, which tracks news and prices including some auction results and direct sales at shows.

There are even some special magazines for hunting and fishing collectibles, black ethnic collectibles, beer cans, and brewery collectibles.

On *World Newspapers.Com* you can find a growing list of online periodicals on every subject—try this and look under "collecting."

## OH, YES, THERE ARE STILL PRINT MAGAZINES . . .

Don't forget the bricks-and-mortar version of your old-fashioned newsstand. Many collectibles magazines in print are not yet available online.

Coin and stamp price guide publishers issue regular updates to their guides in magazine form such as *Coin Values and Scott's Stamp Monthly*, *Linn's*, and *Stamp Magazine*.

*Beckett's* is a source for baseball card and other sports collectible info and publishes several monthlies. *Doll Reader* has a website but only selected content from the monthly print issues is available.

## RETAILERS AND "PORTALS"

A "**portal**" is a website that might be considered an information "**hub**" with links that can take you to other related sites. Try a few of them such as *Curioscape* and *World Collectors Net*.

Many **online dealers** also operate interactive sites with research materials and links on their sites for collectors. Some dealers also offer free appraisals and identification services. Clicking on these sites is much like walking into a store; you can browse the inventory, get some information, possibly ask a question, or show a photograph, even if you are hundreds or thousands of miles from this dealer's place of business!

The *BBC* and *About.Com* also have extensive materials about antiques and collecting, which you can access from their respective home pages.

The internet cannot magically identify a piece for you based on key-words typed into a search engine—that site of the future has yet to be developed!

## SHOWS, FAIRS, AND MALLS

One of the best ways to get information about antiques and collectibles is to see them in person, not just in pictures, and find out how they are priced and why.

Attending an **antique, art, jewelry, or collectibles show or fair** is a good way to do this. You will meet a variety of dealers and ask questions about their items. Don't be afraid, they are used to it! Not every dealer at a show will be friendly or have time to talk, but usually you will find a few who are willing to share their expertise.

Attending shows can help you start to train your own eye to recognize the subtle differences that separate old from new, higher quality from lesser, one designer or maker from another. You will be surprised how quickly you can learn to notice little details when someone points them out to you, and when you see a wide array of items for comparisons.

**Antique malls** often have good collections of small items such as cos-tume jewelry, memorabilia, lamps, clocks, toys, and collectible objects. Space at malls is rented from the management by the dealers, who are not always on hand to answer questions, but sometimes you can find an expert among the mall managers who has seen and handled a lot of collectibles. Malls of-ten maintain a library of price guides, and are usually friendly about helping you learn to browse them.

## ONE SALE IS NOT THE SAME AS ANOTHER

Finding out that something that may be like your item sold for a certain price is NOT a guarantee that your item will sell for the same amount. Far from it! Remember that fine details of rarity and quality, plus the sometimes-unfathomable deviations in collector demand, influence value dramatically.

Dedicated professionals spend lifetimes exploring the beauty and other special qualities of rare and precious items. They study and interact in the marketplace, where prices can swing and soar, bargains can be snapped up, and reputations can be tested.

We can't become instant experts with a click of the mouse—but our rapidly changing world can bring more information than ever before to our fingertips.

So now, let's take a close-up look at some of the most common categories of treasures we might have, and find out how to learn more about them.

# 5

# FURNITURE

Gail grew up in New England during the 1960s. Her mother Doris was a devotee of antiques who collected many pieces of large furniture and small household objects. Doris always referred to her objects as "Early American." She was interested in crafts and took refinishing and stenciling classes.

When Doris passed away, Gail assumed she had inherited a valuable collection of period pieces. She solicited the help of Joan, an antique dealer and appraiser who had been referred to her by the local historical society.

The day Joan arrived to begin the process of appraising the collection, she knew Gail was going to be disappointed. Several of the largest pieces of furniture were indeed crafted of old wood, and looked like Colonial antiques, but Joan could tell that the pieces had been assembled in the twentieth century. She also saw the array of chairs and smaller objects that Doris had refinished and painted, vastly reducing their potential value even though a few of them were from the eighteenth century. She gently explained some of the details to Gail.

"Did Mother know this? That many of these pieces weren't old?" Gail wondered.

"I'm sure she did. There were several workshops in this area that produced these. The craftsmen were not trying to fool anyone—they were turning old wood and pieces that had been thrown away into lovely, affordable decorator pieces."

"But what if someone didn't know where they came from? Wouldn't they assume the furniture was of the period? How can you tell?"

Joan led Gail over to a cherrywood sideboard and opened one of the small top drawers. She examined the area where the sides of the drawer met the front.

"You see the dovetails here, the little triangular pieces where the two sides meet? They are cut in the manner that old drawers were assembled, but the pins and tails are of equal size, as if cut by machine. Also look at the wood used to make the sides of the drawer. They match the front. In a period piece from the seventeenth or eighteenth century the drawer sides would have been from a different wood. Also the sides and front of the drawer are just very slightly thinner and finer than a piece from the period would have. The hardware, the drawer pulls, are also just very slightly later in style. They probably came from an early-nineteenth-century factory, although they look good on this piece."

Gail looked crestfallen. Joan was sorry for her disappointment.

"We can sell many of these pieces through a decorator I know. Shall I just take a look through the rest of the house? Maybe there's something else? Why don't you come with me?"

Gail led Joan through the rest of the house. In an upstairs guest room Joan bent to examine a pair of small mahogany upholstered chairs.

"This is a lovely pair of chairs. How long have you had these?"

"Oh, those. They're old, but they weren't Mother's taste. They came from my father's grandmother's home in New York. Mother kept them in the sewing room. She never let us sit on them, I remember that. They're mahogany and don't go with anything. I keep meaning to give them away."

Joan was unable to hide her smile at Gail's still-dejected tone.

"I'd like to have a friend of mine who is an expert on Duncan Phyfe examine these. The finish looks original to me, and they are in remarkable condition."

"Duncan Phyfe? I thought all that was reproduction."

"Not if it's of the period. These might be valuable, especially if we can trace their origin."

Gail was astounded when her overlooked Duncan Phyfe chairs were appraised at $30,000 by a local appraiser. Joan felt they might sell for more than that if placed in an auction with other important early American furniture. The pair eventually sold for over $42,000. Several of Doris's reproduction pieces were sold through a local decorator. Gail invested in several research books and began to visit antique shops and shows to learn more about the valuable clues to furniture she herself had not known to look for.

"I'll always love and value Mother's things because they were hers," she told me. " I've learned so much from this, and started to collect on my own. One important thing is not to be influenced by your own tast—you can miss something of quality. Another is—never refinish or decorate an old piece, because it can drastically reduce the value."

## ABOUT FURNITURE

Furniture presents special obvious challenges. For one thing it can be big and heavy! You can't just toss it into the back of the SUV and haul it over to the local antique shop for a free evaluation. Neither does it pack neatly into boxes for efficient storage.

Furniture is also a tricky asset to identify correctly. Even a seasoned expert here and there can be fooled or perplexed when it comes to determining the age of a piece. Most popular styles of antique furniture have been widely reproduced down through the centuries.

To value furniture correctly, something about its age must be known.

## IMPORTANT STYLES OF ANTIQUE FURNITURE

Furniture is categorized by its style, age, and country of origin. Some names refer to the original *designers*, such as **Chippendale** and **Hepplewhite**, both cabinetmakers in eighteenth-century England, producing most of their designs around the 1750s–1780s. Other furniture is called by the *name of the* *historical period* when it was first designed, such as **Louis XV, Empire, Regency, Georgian**. Some furniture is called after the *area* in which it was commonly made, such as **French Provincial**, or by the crafts movement in which the style first emerged, such as **Shaker, Arts and Crafts**, or "**Biedermeier**," an artistic period in early-nineteenth-century Vienna, characterized by the use of light fruitwoods, burl veneers, and simple, graceful, curving lines.

In the Victorian Era, which began around 1830 and lasted until nearly the end of the nineteenth century, many popular styles of the past were revived and reproduced extensively. Some particularly popular styles include the florid **Rococo**, with ornate decorative carving; **Jacobean**; and **Renaissance Revival**, with its massive, boxy lines. Many different furniture styles were re-created in factories in the later nineteenth and twentieth centuries.

For many years, seventeenth- and eighteenth-century European and English furniture was traditionally considered the most valuable. Much true European furniture from these periods is in museums. Recently, Early American furniture has begun to increase in importance and desirability among collectors. Some furniture experts believe continental and English furniture may actually have become undervalued, when compared to the lofty American prices.

---

### AT AUCTION

The world auction record holder for American furniture was a **Chippendale** block and shell carved desk and bookcase, c. 1760–1770, attributed to **John Goddard**, which sold at Christie's in 1989 for $12.1 million.

At Skinner's in November 2004, a **lacquered Boston maple and pine chest** skyrocketed to $1,876,000, well exceeding its estimate of $300–500,000.

---

Besides Early American, collectors lately have been turning their attention to some very specific, and more recent, movements in furniture, creating some surprising shifts in furniture values.

## ART NOUVEAU—ARTS AND CRAFTS

The **Art Nouveau** movement took place from the early 1890s until around 1920. Art Nouveau was characterized by imaginative, sometimes fanciful designs and encompassed furniture, glass, and other decorative arts.

Around the time of Art Nouveau, which might be said to be an artistic movement taking place in the cities, a "back to simplicity" development was taking place in rural America, a movement now called **Arts and Crafts**. One of the most famous names associated with the Arts and Crafts period is that of the **Stickley** family. The five Stickley brothers—Gustav, Leopold, J. G., Albert, and Charles started their family furniture company in Binghamton, New York, in 1880. But the Stickley name was passed on to several future generations of family business partners, and furniture is still being manufactured today in the Stickley name.

Another craftsman of the period was Elbert **Hubbard**, who started the **Roycroft** craft community in upstate New York around the turn of the twentieth century. Influenced by the philosophy and designs of **William Morris**, Hubbard advocated quality and simplicity. His workshop produced much sturdy oak and mahogany furniture and also lamps, frames, and other small items.

During the 1890–1930 period much inexpensive oak furniture was made in styles similar to Arts and Crafts. Design elements from certain styles of the past were brought in too. This period is sometimes called **"Mission"** or **"Bungalow"** style in California, and elsewhere "country oak" or "golden oak." Especially in the West and Midwest, towns were growing, and people needed relatively inexpensive, no-frills, sturdy furniture around the house. This type of furniture was sold in Sears catalogs and by other well-known retailers around the country.

Wicker, bentwood, and bamboo furniture also was popular during this turn of the century period. It was lightweight and somewhat inexpensive to manufacture. The **Thonet** company, started by designer Michael Thonet in Austria in the 1850s, was one of the best-known manufacturers of bentwood furniture, especially chairs. Wicker and rattan, which is the material from which wicker furniture is made, are a little less popular now than they were in the later part of the twentieth century, and because the materials are sensitive to the environment, they are harder to find in perfect condition.

## DARLING DECO AND MARVELOUS MODERN

The **Art Deco** movement, from around 1925 to the 1940s, was characterized by angular or geometric shapes, sleek lines, exotic and inlaid woods, and theatrical motifs.

Deco was inspired and influenced by Hollywood, King Tut's tomb, and the cubist art movement.

In the 1920s a new furniture revolution now called **Modern** began to evolve. One of the early pioneers of this movement was Hungarian-born **Marcel Breuer**, who designed one of the first tubular steel chairs for the living room in 1925.

The Modern period brought startling new designs in modern materials, chrome and leather, and stark, unusual shapes and colors. Some of the more famous Modern designers were **Le Corbusier**, **Eero Saarinen**, **Mies Van Der Rohe**, **Charles Eames**, **George Nelson**, **George Nakashima**, and **Isamu Noguchi**. Several influential furniture manufacturers such as **Herman Miller** and **Knoll** rose to importance through their distribution of the designs of the artists of this period.

## FURNITURE VALUES

Furniture, like other antiques and collectibles, varies greatly in price depending on condition, the current popularity of a particular style, and provenance. Style, desirability, and condition may factor more importantly than exact age. Even at auction, where many details about the age and origin of the piece will be written into its description, there is not necessarily a rule that a piece from circa 1910 is worth less than one from 1890, or for that matter a piece from 1927 worth less than one from 1886.

As with fine art, **important museum exhibitions** can boost a furniture maker's popularity.

The work of French Art Deco designer **Jacques-Emile Ruhlmann** was featured in a 2004 museum show that traveled to the Metropolitan Museum of Art in New York, increasing demand for the designer's already sought-after lamps, desks, and cabinets.

Conversely, **quantities of reproductions** could depress the appeal of some designers—this may dampen prices of some popular Modern furniture artists, as the popularity of famous Modern designers is creating a boom in replicas.

---

## AT AUCTION

A 1948 glass and oak trestle table by Italian designer **Carlo Mollino** sold for $3.8 million at Christie's in June 2005. At Wright in Chicago, an **Isamu Noguchi** marble table brought $630,000 in December 2005. A chrome and lacquer desk by **Jacques-Emile Ruhlmann** tied the world record for a Deco object at Christie's in 2000, going for a hammer price of $1,876,000.

---

Closer to earth, one of the highest priced items in *Krause's 2002 Furniture Field Guide* was a set of **Johannes Hansen** Danish Modern chairs, c. 1949, priced at $28,750. A pair of late-eighteenth-century Federal mahogany side chairs from Massachusetts was listed at $23,000.

## WHAT THE EXPERT KNOWS

Furniture is possibly the asset that requires the highest degree of connoisseurship to evaluate correctly. Get several opinions, and provide as much information as possible about the history of the piece in order to get the most complete evaluation.

An expert who looks at your furniture will look for certain signs and details, like a detective looking for clues to a crime. He will be finely attuned to *stylistic* elements and especially proportions; some very slight *design variations* can distinguish a reproduction to his eye. Marks from the use of various *tools* that were available to carve and saw wood at different periods will help him date the piece.

An expert knows the differences between seventeenth- or eighteenth-century carving and more modern versions. He will also know:

the look of *patina* of older woods
the slight variances in weight and color of woods that were commonly used in different periods

the thickness of veneers used in different periods

the look of antique joints and dovetails, the thickness of boards, how the backs of legs might be more roughly finished

how to interpret signatures, stamps, and manufacturer's labels, hardware, screws, and nails

Subtle signs of wear to the areas of the piece where it has been handled, and affects of exposure to the wood from sun or humidity will also give clues to age, as will evidence of repairs, and of typical damage from use.

## FURNITURE LINGO

Armoire—free standing wardrobe

Bergere—large upholstered armchair

Bombe—convex or bulge-shaped front, usually of a chest

Boulle—style named for a master seventeenth-century designer using decorative veneers of tortoise-shell, brass, and other inlaid materials

Cabriole—double curved shape for legs and feet

Cheval—not a horse—but a mirror with a base, sometimes free-standing

Commode—a type of wide, low chest with two or three drawers

Etagere—free-standing shelf

Festoon—a carved decorative element

Ormolu—gilt-covered brass used for decoration

Recamier—a type of sofa or recliner

Repousse—a design in relief

Secretary—a desk with a bookcase top

Veneer—thin layer of wood glued to less expensive wood base

Wallace Nutting—a craftsman famous for reproduction American furniture from 1917 to the 1940s

## FIND OUT ABOUT FURNITURE

Check out the *University of Delaware's Furniture Library*, which offers articles, links, an A–Z antique guide, and a reference bookshelf. *The Carnegie*

*Library* of Pittsburgh has a bibliography of furniture price guides, directories of makers, and reference books about styles.

**Furniture style guides** can help you with illustrations and explanations of antique periods and styles. I have not found too many extensive ones yet online; *Connected Lines* has software you can download. Several sites are style-specific; *American Decorative Arts*' website has extensive modern furniture resources, including catalogs from the 1920s through the 1980s.

**Furniture price guides** are useful, but may not help you as much with pricing as they will for some other collectible assets. If you browse through a few you'll notice that prices vary in the extreme, and the identification points do not always add up to a complete description of a piece.

## WHAT TO DO WITH YOUR FURNITURE

Valuable furniture should be kept safe from heat, moisture, dirt, strong sunlight, and other potential hazards. If you don't have much room, find a storage facility where you can have access to show the furniture to potential buyers or appraisers.

You can dust furniture if it's dirty. Don't use polish or oils, remove or alter finishes, or try to clean upholstery stains yourself. Don't try to make repairs—you can reinforce a loose board or cracked leg with masking tape for the time being.

## WHERE DID IT COME FROM?

Remember your catalog? Make a list of your furniture with as many **details** as you can concerning the history, or provenance of the items. Receipts, letters, notes, or old family photos that you may find can be useful in dating and establishing origin of furniture.

Look for clues to age by examining whether there are **dowels** (wooden pegs), nails, screws, or dovetails (the line of triangular or square wedges used to fasten boards together at corners). What about the surface of the wood? Is it chipped, smooth, pitted, or bumpy? Are there signs of years of wear—water stains, rings, edges worn round or smooth? Are chair legs bumped and dinged or new-looking?

Search the piece for **manufacturer's marks** on the backs and undersides. Check backs of the pieces—are they finished or unfinished? Is there a lightweight board nailed onto the back of a dresser? Are the backs of legs finished or rough? Examine nails, screws, and hardware—do you see any marked with a cross, like a Phillips head screw? Older pieces will have nails and screws with only one indentation like a single line. Is the hardware lightweight or heavy? Finely made with signs of machine stamping? All of these checkpoints can be clues to age.

Some of this scrutiny is more important with furniture than with other antiques. Why? Because furniture can't be easily moved, a more detailed description will enable you to share it with possible buyers or auction houses who cannot see it readily. A local dealer, appraiser, expert from a museum or historical society, or staff person from a regional auction company can give you an opinion of the age and quality of a piece, but having the most detailed information possible will enable you to inquire about it *knowledgeably* at a distance.

Eighteenth-century antique furniture, and authentic examples of the important periods and styles we listed above, should be sold through major and regional auction companies. Smaller local auction companies can evaluate Victorian reproductions, country oak, wrought iron, wicker, quality twentieth-century furniture, and reproduction modern furniture. We'll discuss auctions and different types of auction companies in chapter 15.

## IF IT'S NOT A RARE ANTIQUE...

Contemporary furniture of the type you can purchase in furniture store chains may not be considered salable to collectors, even if it is in a traditional or antique style. Fine-quality designer pieces may be marketable through decorators, or possibly consigned or sold to specialty dealers. You can consider trying to market this type of furniture yourself through **classified ads** or at a **yard sale** or an **estate sale,** or through a local auction liquidator or estate broker. Some cities may also have **consignment shops** or **furniture resale stores**—check your Yellow Pages or local online community pages.

> *Selling Tip*: Furniture is not one of the biggest items on eBay, but many sellers offer pickup or local delivery to buyers in the area. If you need to ship furniture, contact a specialized freight company that has experience in antiques for estimates before quoting shipping costs.

If your furniture does not have a high degree of collectible value, there might be opportunities to sell it for decorative purposes. Hotels, restaurants, bars, and bed-and-breakfasts may be looking for "vintage" furniture in antique styles. The prop and set departments of movie companies may be interested in period pieces of different kinds.

Furniture that may not be salable can be donated to charities who will put it to good use in shelters, halfway houses, hospitals, rehab centers, or community centers. Charities will usually pick up the furniture from you and give you a receipt. Another idea is to offer it to a community theater company, or the drama department of a local high school or college for use in set design. You'll find out more about **donations** in chapter 17.

# 6

# CERAMICS AND GLASS

Possibly no area of collecting is as extensive, and therefore as daunting, as ceramics and glass. The good news is, museums, galleries, collector clubs, research societies, websites, reference books, fairs, trade shows, software, and classes are devoted to these cherished items!

**Supply and demand** is important where values of china and glass are concerned. Fine dinnerware and glassware are still manufactured in large quantities, so many antique pieces as well as those of more recent vintage have variable resale values. Commanding top prices are eighteenth- and very early nineteenth-century porcelain, important designer names such as Tiffany and Lalique, and signed pieces of Arts and Crafts pottery. But many different types of china and glass items are valuable and sought-after in this vast market.

## CHINA AND PORCELAIN—WHAT'S THE DIFFERENCE?

Both porcelain and pottery are made from clay as a starting point. Pottery usually has a coarser, possibly heavier appearance than porcelain, and may be opaque when held to the light. The two main types of pottery are **earthenware** and **stoneware**, which are fired at different temperatures.

Porcelain may be either **hard-paste**—brilliant and hard, or **soft-paste**—more porous. Most porcelain is decorated with pigment or enamel, which can be applied before or after the piece is glazed. Early porcelain was painted by hand; many modern pieces are also decorated this way.

Porcelain is thought to have been invented by the Chinese around the sixth century AD. The art was secret for many centuries. It was not until nearly 1500 that the first Japanese porcelain was made, and Dutch exploration ships brought the items back to Europe from the Orient.

During the Italian Renaissance of the 1500s, the first soft-paste European porcelain was manufactured, and experiments were soon underway in England and France to replicate the hard-paste quality of the Far Eastern treasures. It was a German physicist and mathematician, Ehrenfried Walter, and a young man named Johann Friedrich Bottger, who had dabbled in alchemy, who put their geological research and artistic talents together to establish the first important Germain porcelain factory at **Meissen** in the early 1700s.

**Sevres** was the most important French porcelain factory in the eighteenth century. Under the direct supervision of King Louis XV, some of the finest pieces in the world were made. A bright "robin's egg" blue color characterizes some Sevres pieces, and many were decorated with gold or bronze.

In England, one of the most famous potteries was established by **Josiah Wedgewood** in 1759. Although Wedgewood produced pottery in several finishes and styles, the two- or three-colored **jasperware** is the most famous, and is still being made today. Also in England, around 1794, a type of porcelain was developed that came to be called "**bone china**," using a high proportion of bone ash to the clay ingredients.

## POTTERY—ART OF THE ANCIENTS

While porcelain has been widely produced only in the last few centuries, the history of pottery dates back to several thousand years BC. The concept of *artistic* pottery, however, is a relatively modern one. Art pottery is considered to have its origins in America and Britain around the late nineteenth century, along with the rise of the **Arts and Crafts** movement. The pottery school at **Sophie Newcomb College** in New Orleans, started in 1895, is considered to have influenced the development of modern art pottery in the United

States. Arts and Crafts pottery blossomed during the period from around 1885 to the early 1930s, and is a very important collectible area today. Some of the major designers and manufacturers include **William Moorcroft, Rookwood, Marblehead, Weller, Wheatley,** and **Grueby. Teco** is a name that refers to the American Terra Cotta and Ceramic Company, which manufactured an art pottery line with a green matte glaze until the early 1920s.

Decorative ceramic **tiles,** made for tea tables, fireplaces, floors, and walls are also sought-after from this period.

Pottery is a medium that has always attracted artists as well as craftsmen. Today the works of major ceramic artists such as **Beatrice Wood** and **Peter Voulkos** sell for prices into the thousands.

## WHY IS IT CALLED...?

Pottery and porcelain can be named:

> for an **area, region, or city** such as **Limoges, Staffordshire, Nippon,** and **Delft,** or **Quimper, Meissen, Roseville (Ohio),** or **Darby**
> for a **specific factory or company,** such as **Grueby, McCoy,** or **Hull**
> for an **artist or designer** such as the Hungarian **Vilmos Zsolnay,** who influenced the Art Nouveau movement
> for **styles, color, or descriptions** such as "**Mocha,**" "**Flow Blue,**" "**Blue and White,**" or brightly colored **Fiesta**

Common **Oriental** styles of porcelain include the gilt-tinged, intricate **Satsuma,** produced in Japan since the eighteenth century; **Imari,** with typical blue and orange colors and medallion type designs, and the **Chinese Rose Canton** and **Rose Medallion.**

Many famous factories of the past such as **Wedgewood, Royal Doulton, Royal Copenhagen, Lenox, Hall,** and **Minton** are still manufacturing today, making it easy for all but the expert collector to become confused over the exact age of a piece.

## IDENTIFYING CERAMIC PIECES

Most pottery and porcelain is "**marked**" or **signed** with an emblem, name, symbol, or design to signify the manufacturer. In many cases the age and producer of the piece can be determined by a careful examination of the underside of the object and a detailed study and comparison of the mark that is found. There are hundreds, if not thousands, of ceramic marks, and fortunately the marks of most important manufacturers have been cataloged. Many company marks, for example **Royal Worcester** or **Royal Bayreuth**, will bear the name spelled out. Some, like **Meissen** and **Royal Copenhagen**, will use a symbol—in their cases a pair of crossed swords, or three wavy lines—sometimes in conjunction with their name, sometimes not. Over centuries marks have been altered during different periods, making it possible for the ceramics expert—or good student—to learn to date a piece from the history of the marks used by the company. You can buy a directory of porcelain and pottery marks, find one at a library, or sometimes browse through one at an antique store.

Deborah bought a set of four seven-inch blue-and-white dishes for $5.00 in the 1970s, and wondered if they had any value. They were marked "Woods Ware—Old Bow—Kakiyemon," which she thought was an odd name for an obviously English pattern.

We decided to conduct an internet search together to see what we could find out about her dishes. We were easily able to learn that Woods was a British Staffordshire pottery company formed in 1865, and that it had still existed into the 1980s.

Thanks to Beauville Antiques' "Collectors Corner" website, I learned that this Japanese-inspired pattern had been produced from 1922 to 1929 by Woods and designed by Frederick Rhead, Woods' art director. Now, I could search for some examples of Old Bow Kakiyemon, of which there were not many. I found a partial set with creamers, platters, dining plates, and tureens with an asking price of $350, with the individual pieces priced between $10 and $35. On eBay I found a gravy boat with a starting bid of around $5, and a meat platter on another auction site starting at $3.79.

What did we learn from this?

We were able to identify the pieces as to manufacturer, designer, and probable date, and find out a little about the state of their market.

While Deborah's pieces seemed somewhat scarce, they were obviously not on every Staffordshire collector's wish list! They would **probably** not sell for more than a few dollars, unless someone was looking for them specifically, for instance to complete a set.

## ABOUT GLASS

Glass has been made for thousands of years. Archaeologists have discovered pieces that date back to 3500 BC or earlier. The basic material of glass is **quartz**, found in sand or silica, which is heated to an extremely high temperature. Glass objects are formed and shaped by either blowing or molding. During the Roman Empire the process of blowing was invented and refined.

In 1676 an Englishman named George Ravenscroft added lead oxide to a mixture of glass composite resulting in a brighter, more sparkling glass still referred to as "**lead crystal**."

Glass has been commonly overlaid with gilt, etched, or decorated with enamel.

"Cut" glass was first made using stone or metal wheels. During the nineteenth and twentieth centuries, the process of cut glassmaking by machines developed in stages. The first cut glass in America was produced around 1771 in a Pennsylvania factory started by Henry William Stiegel. At first American glass was made in the fashion of English, Irish, and Continental European wares, but a flowering of ingenuity and creativity began to influence the glass industry in the early and middle 1800s. The "American Brilliant Cut Glass" period (the later 1800s through the end of World War I) produced some of the most excellent craftsmanship in glass.

"**Pressed**" glass was first made in the United States after the 1820s, when glass pressing machines were invented. When you have seen and identified pressed glass, you will usually know it when you see it again. The patterns are often delicate and intricate and look like they have been stamped or molded onto the glass.

## WHY IS IT CALLED...?

Glass, like porcelain and pottery, may be named:

for its **manufacturer** (Baccarat or Steuben)
for the **location of a principal factory** (Waterford)
for a particular **region**, such as Venetian glass, or Murano, an island off the coast of Venice. Murano glass originated in the thirteenth century; the name is used today to refer to contemporary glass manufactured on the island.

for a **particular pattern or color** such as Cranberry, Custard Glass, Milk, and Peachblow.

Some famous glass names are particularly confusing.

**Sandwich Glass** refers to glass made by a specific factory, the Boston and Sandwich Company, between 1825 and 1888, but there were many different types and styles of glass in the factory's repertoire. Since Boston and Sandwich was one of the first pressed glass manufacturers, much Sandwich glass might also be referred to as pressed glass! Items from other glass factories such as Cape Cod Glassworks, which operated in the town of Sandwich, might also be considered "Sandwich glass." To complicate matters further, a particular glass pattern manufactured by several unrelated glass companies in the 1920s was also called "Sandwich."

**"Bohemian"** glass refers to an ornate overlay glass made first in Czechoslovakia and popular during the Victorian era in the United States.

**"Cambridge"** was an Ohio company founded around the turn of the century whose elegant etched and colored styles, popular in the 1920s–1940s, include **Crown Tuscan** and **Rosepoint**.

**"Swarovski,"** known for Austrian crystal "par excellence," was founded in 1895 and is famous for animal figurines, candlesticks, and other decorative accessories.


## TIFFANY AND ART NOUVEAU GLASS

Several glass artists came to prominence during the late nineteenth century during the **Art Nouveau** period. Two of the most important were **Rene Lalique** and **Louis Comfort Tiffany**. Lalique designed in Paris from the 1890s until around 1945. He was famous for his elegant perfume bottles, fanciful animal figures, and delicate satin-like finish. Tiffany, who worked in New York from 1879 to the 1930s, pioneered the use of acids and metal oxides to give glass an iridescent hue. Tiffany was a craftsman who worked in bronze, pottery, and silver as well as glass. He is perhaps most famous for his leaded-glass lamps but produced a vast number of important vases, bowls, compotes, and other accessories.

**Emile Galle, Philip Handel, Johann Loetz, and the Daum brothers, Auguste and Jean-Antonin**, were other important Art Nouveau glass artists. Signed pieces by major artists can fetch prices in the tens of thousands, but many pieces of art glass from this period sell in the high hundreds or low thousands. As with other antiques, craftsmanship, originality, rarity, quality of design, and execution are factors in determining value.

---

## AT AUCTION

Tiffany's beautiful Art Nouveau floral lamps have always been popular, but have recently achieved stratospheric prices. At Sotheby's June 2005 Twentieth Century Design sale, a Peony table lamp brought down the hammer at $576,000.

Art Pottery sales are strong. In 2000, a rare Marblehead vase signed with the initials of its artist, Hannah Tutt, and originally estimated to sell for around $15,000, brought over $120,000 at Rago Auctions.

In 2005, an aqua blown glass jar estimated at $3–500 sold for $1762.50 at Skinner's. The jar contained a note inside that identified the jar's early-nineteenth-century New Hampshire factory.

---

## CARNIVAL AND DEPRESSION GLASS

Because of its beauty and desirability, several companies manufactured less expensive forms of "imitation" Art Nouveau decorative glass around the turn of the century and into the 1930s. Two of the most common, still growing in popularity with collectors today, are Carnival glass and Depression glass. Both are a form of molded pressed glass.

Carnival glass, which is still being made today, was created by shaping a small amount of molten glass and then spraying it with a liquid mixture of metallic salts before firing. This gives the glass an iridescent look of many flowing colors.

There are over a thousand different Carnival glass patterns and several major colors, including marigold, amethyst, deep blue, red, and amber. There were five major Carnival glass factories—Northwood, Fenton, Imperial, Dugan, and Millersberg—and of these only Fenton is still in operation. Part of the mystique of Carnival glass is that many original molds have been lost or destroyed, making certain patterns irreplaceable.

The Carnival glass collecting world was rocked in 2003 when an unusual Carnival glass plate sold on eBay for over $16,000. The plate was a **Northwood Strawberry** pattern in a very unusual Ice Blue color—only four plates were known to have been manufactured in that color. Most Carnival glass is much less expensive. Nice pieces can be bought for less than a hundred dollars. More important examples sell for into the $1–3,000 range.

Depression glass is inexpensive patterned clear and colored tableware that was widely manufactured in the 1920s and 1930s. There were many manufacturers, among them **Anchor-Hocking, Hocking, Hazel-Atlas, Indiana Glass Company, Jeannette Glass**, and **Westmoreland**.

Until recently you could find Depression glass easily at flea markets and thrift stores, and probably still can! It is a good example of an ordinary household object that has now become a collectible, gaining in price and popularity.

## MODERN AND CONTEMPORARY GLASS

"Studio glass" refers to one-of-a-kind sculptures by glass artists. Some major glass factories such as **Baccarat** and the Swiss manufacturer **Orrefors** manufacture high-quality decorative pieces. **Steuben** glass is still in business today but manufactures clear glass only.

## WHAT THE EXPERT KNOWS

The **ceramics expert** will know what decorative touches were used at different times, and what colors and patterns are characteristic of selected periods. He or she will study wear, especially on handles or on the bottom of a dish, and perhaps the thickness or style of any base or rim around the bottom of the piece. "Crazing," a crackling of the glaze, can sometimes be a clue to the age of a piece of pottery, but many twentieth-century pieces have also been deliberately crazed, and the expert will have seen examples of both kinds.

The expert sees hairline cracks, chips, and other signs of damage or usage, and hidden signs of repair. He or she will examine the marks or any signatures that may be present, and pay attention to the weight or even the sound of the piece when tapped, all for clues to age and quality of materials. The expert will know hand-painting from decal, and when some styles have been reproduced. He will know the details of color, ornamentation and design used in different periods, by different artists, even at different factories. One porcelain collector told me he can sometimes tell in what country a piece is made just by the colors of the glazes, although the variances are subtle.

A **glass expert** will study the *style, lines, and shape* of the design, and the color, texture, and appearance of the glass as it reflects and absorbs light. He will look for imperfections such as air bubbles, minor chips, imperceptible cracks, and any designer's or maker's marks not easily visible to the untrained eye. The weight and "feel" of the glass in his hand will provide clues to its possible origins; valuable glass may be lighter and more fragile. Other indicators of value and vintage may be found in the *etching or carving designs* on the glass, gilt, or other decoration. He will easily be able to identify a unique, hand-crafted piece from a mass-produced one.

## CERAMICS AND GLASS LINGO

Fortunately, unlike furniture, pieces of pottery and porcelain are described by English names of objects that are generally easy to understand—pitcher, bowl, and so forth. But there are literally hundreds, if not thousands, of terms to describe origins, styles, and techniques. A few of the most general include:

Amphora—a two-handled vase

Bevel—glass edge ground and polished at an angle

Bone China—durable white translucent ware made with bone ash, developed by **Josiah Spode** in late-eighteenth-century London. Spode's factory, founded in 1770, still bears his name today

Blanc de Chine—white glazed porcelain in the style of late-seventeenth- and eighteenth-century Chinese ware

Capo di Monte—porcelain with decorative molded relief in a style that originated in Naples in 1743

Export Ware—general term for sixteenth- to twentieth-century ceramics manufactured in China and Japan for sale abroad

Faience—French term for tin-glazed earthenware, similarly called Delft (Holland) or Majolica (Italy)

Glaze—general term for vitreous (glass-like) coating fired onto the surface of a piece

Jardiniere—flower pot

Jasperware—unglazed, opaque stoneware colored all the way through, often with contrasting white cameo bas-relief ornamentation— introduced by Josiah Wedgewood in 1775

Leaded Glass—sheet glass pieces joined with metal strips—OR—glass with a lead content

Millefiore—an Italian term meaning "thousand flowers" used to describe mosaic glass

Studio Glass—one-of-a-kind pieces made by glass artists

Terrazo—a combination of marble, granite, onyx, or glass chips in cement

## CERAMICS AND GLASS VALUES

Price guides for ceramics should list by manufacturer, as well as by style and period. Some interesting and pricey items in *The Antique Trader's Ceramics Price Guide—4th Edition* included nineteenth- and twentieth-century vases from the **Teplitz** region of Bohemia, now the Czech Republic, many ranging from $1500 to $5000. Among the highest priced items in the guide were several rare **Newcomb** vases ranging from $17,000 to over $46,000.

**Limoges** pieces—not a specific maker but a generic name for the region of France where many important factories were based—were also showing significant value; several *jardinieres* (flower pots) were priced in the $3000 range, with tea, punch, and chocolate sets, serving platters, and vases also among the highest priced.

Early English and French **egg cups,** by contrast, were priced from $15 to $40. **Hull** cookie jars, creamers, vases, and animal figurines ranged from $30 to $300.

Much china found in estates will be sets of dinnerware and accompanying serving pieces. On an ordinary day I found over 161,000 eBay listings in the Dinnerware category, subdivided into well over a hundred manufacturers. To get a feeling for the marketplace for your china, you must first identify the maker and the pattern, and then browse the category or look for comparable items on retail sites.

Art glass can be priced variably, depending on the importance of the designer, as well as the quality and craftsmanship of a specific piece. At a recent antique show, I saw a stunning Loetz vase with an asking price of $900 and a decorated Burmese jar with gilt highlights for $1200. Judith Miller's *2004 Collectibles Price Guide* had several small signed Galle jars in the $4–700 range, priced (surprisingly) lower than several unsigned 1980s Murano vases.

Sometimes an unusual item will bring an unexpectedly high price: a paperweight made of light green translucent "vaseline" glass was priced at $1200 in an antique shop I visited recently. Glass has to be thought of as an art and design item—it is almost like the fine art market in that styles, designers, and periods can come and go from fashion.

## FIND OUT ABOUT CERAMICS AND GLASS

You can look for a ceramics or glass expert at a major or regional auction company, or a decorative arts museum. Wedgewood has hosted evaluation and appraisal clinics at its Stoke-on-Trent factory and visitor center in England. *Ceramics Today* magazine has book reviews, collector resources, and dealer links. The *Corning Glass Museum* has a library and other research for glass and fine art. *Rago Arts* is a specialized auction company in Lambertville, New Jersey, founded by an American art pottery expert. The **Morse Museum of American Art** in Winter Park, Florida, houses an important Tiffany collection.

*Replacements* has over 200,000 china patterns on its website. If you know the name of the pattern and manufacturer, you can view a picture and see what pieces are being offered for sale. The site also offers free **identification services** for a minimum of items.

Many collectors' clubs have information services, and some online retailers offer identification services where you can submit a digital photo and description of your item, sometimes for a small fee. Try typing some descriptive words into eBay's advanced search page, or post a query with a digital photo on the Pottery, Glass, and Porcelain category discussion board. You can also see a lot of porcelain and glass at an antique show or at a local antique mall.

## HOW TO RESEARCH MARKS

Of the hundreds of reference guides in print, there is probably one that details the marks and dates of the manufacturer of your china. One site you can go to is **Bradshaw and Whelan Reference Books** to see a rather extensive list, as well as information on restoration services. For a more general guidebook, Ralph and Terry Kovel have *Kovel's New Dictionary of Marks* (Random House Reference, 1986), or see Chad Lage's *Pictorial Guide to Pottery and Porcelain Marks* (Collector Books, 2004).

You can find these on new and used book sites or at the public library, or you can often browse through one at an antique store. The **International Ceramic Directory** has an extensive list of links to mark-identification sites online.

## WHAT TO DO WITH CERAMICS AND GLASS

Examine each piece carefully to see if it is marked, stamped, numbered, signed, or inscribed. Save any materials that may provide clues to age and history of the articles. Go through any boxes or packing materials that may be present to look for receipts or other clues to the history of the items. Because of the extent to which china and porcelain objects have been reproduced, it will be extremely important for the identification of your pieces to know as much as you can about where and when they were acquired.

Always handle ceramic and glass pieces by the body of the piece, not by an extremity such as a handle. It is okay to clean glass and glazed porcelain *carefully* with a damp cloth and even a little soap and water. Unglazed ceramic ware can be susceptible to staining, so it is best just to pat it with a very lightly dampened cloth, not soak it in water. The dishwasher should not be used. You can dust crevices with a small, clean, dry, paint or makeup brush. Some iridescent glass may be sensitive to hot water and soap, so try a damp, cool rag on it first.

Don't try to repair any cracks or broken pieces, just wrap the pieces together gently in some cloth for storage. Newspaper can cause staining; for packing, use tissue paper around the article first to protect it from the newspaper. Plastic bubble wrap is not a good idea either, since heat could cause it to stick to the articles.

Glass and porcelain are somewhat resilient to light and temperature, but it is never a good idea to store any kind of antique in direct sunlight or, for instance, on top of a radiator. Don't keep glass or crystal in a room with a "surround sound" type stereo system—the vibrations could cause cracking.

Art pottery is in demand almost everywhere now; many auction companies will be interested in evaluating any pieces you may have. For a piece of antique porcelain to be handled by a major auction company, it needs to be something of rare or exceptional quality. A regional auction company will be able to market estate collections of nineteenth- and early-twentieth-century pieces.

An **estate sale** is an excellent way to market pottery, porcelain, and glass, since potential buyers can see the pieces up close and they don't need a big truck to haul their purchases away! China, especially dinnerware, is also one of the most active categories on eBay. Pieces don't have to be sold as a set, either; there is good demand for place settings and individual items.

---

*Selling Tip*: If you sell on eBay, sellers suggest using **double-box** packing for shipping fragile items, wrapping the inner box in bubble wrap so there are no gaps in the package.

---

# 7

# JEWELRY

J anet inherited a beautiful antique necklace and matching pair of ear-
rings from her Aunt Julia. They were made from delicate brushed gold,
adorned with tiny pearls and garnets.

Although she loved the pieces, Janet rarely wore the jewelry, feeling it
was overly formal-looking.

An insurance appraisal had valued the gems at $1200. Janet had a
young daughter and had been thinking of starting a small college fund for
her. One day she took the pieces to a fine jewelry shop in an exclusive area
of town, which had advertised a specialty in estate jewelry. She was shocked
and disappointed at the jeweler's offer—he would buy Aunt Julia's pieces
for $250!

"He said the pearls were small, and that garnets were only semiprecious
stones," Janet recounted. "The pieces dated from the 1920s, which meant
they were newer than what I had thought; but the jeweler said it didn't
matter, that a lot of antique jewelry wasn't really valuable. But why did the
appraiser say they were worth more?"

Jewelry is one of the most common assets we are apt to own or inherit.
But, as Janet found, it can be complicated and confusing to value. Would
you imagine, for instance, that a chunky 1930s bracelet made of Bakelite,

a plastic developed in the early 1900s, would sell for over $3000, while an antique gold and aquamarine brooch might only be worth $250?

Even very fine jewelry can be subject to a variety of opinions as to its fair market value.

In 2004, Consumer Reports conducted an experiment in jewelry valuation. An antique diamond watch appraised by a master gem appraiser, who analyzed the watch stone by stone and determined its value to be $1500. Then four different appraisers were asked to evaluate the watch. Their appraisals ranged from $500 to $3500!

## JEWELRY IN ESTATES

Personal tastes, associations, and memories can make a piece of jewelry more valuable to one person than to another. A surprising number of wills and trusts do not make specific bequests of jewelry or give directions for its disposition. It is not always simple to make equal distributions to multiple heirs.

Many people already have jewelry insured against theft or loss. Any new estate plan or review of an existing plan should include appraisal documents for jewelry and, especially if the collection is valuable, specific instructions for its transfer. As Janet learned, insurance appraisals are not the same as **fair market value appraisals**. The insurance appraisals can help to *identify* the pieces but a new estate appraisal should be made for the purpose of valuation and disposition of a collection.

## HOW TO IDENTIFY FINE JEWELRY

Fine jewelry is generally made of **precious metal**: gold, platinum, or sometimes sterling silver. Costume jewelry is usually made of some kind of **base metal** such as brass, copper, nickel, or steel, and "electroplated" with gold or silver. Gold in its purest form is too soft to be made into most jewelry, so other metals—nickel, zinc, copper, or silver—are added.

A **karat** is a unit of fineness, or gold content. One karat is 1/24 part of pure gold. Fineness may also be expressed as a percentage or in parts per thousand; a metal that is 90% (.900) gold has a fineness of 900.

22-karat gold has a gold content of 91.6% (.916), or 916 parts per thousand

18-karat gold has a gold content of 75% (.750), or 750 parts per thousand

14-karat gold has a gold content of 58.5% (.585), or 585 parts per thousand

**"White gold"** is an alloy of gold, nickel, and zinc. It was developed in 1912, because of the popularity of the more expensive platinum, so if you have a piece of white gold jewelry it is from the twentieth century. White gold can have the same karat content as regular gold.

Gold jewelry is usually stamped or marked with its karat in the United States. British, European, and other foreign jewelers more often mark the piece with the numerical percentage, and sometimes hallmarks to designate the gold content.

**"Gold filled"** refers to a layering or sandwiching of sheets of gold with a sheet of base metal. "*Gold plate*" or "*electroplate*" means the piece is made entirely of base metal and coated with a very thin layer of gold. Electroplating was first used in the 1840s. If you see a mark on a gold piece with the letters "HGE" it refers to "heavy gold electroplate."

The Gold and Silver Stamping Act of 1906 required that all jewelry identified by its gold content be accompanied by a manufacturer's trademark. Prior to this, jewelry was sometimes marked "gold" or even "14-kt," when it was actually gold filled. This means if you have a nineteenth-century piece, the stamping may not be accurate.

## SILVER AND PLATINUM

Pure silver, referred to as .999 pure, is usually mixed with a base metal to be made into jewelry. "*Sterling Silver*" refers to refined silver mixed with a small amount of copper to a percentage of .925 fine, so sterling might be marked either "STER" or .925. Silverplate is similar in its process to gold plating—a thin coating of silver is applied over a base of nickel or copper.

Platinum is usually marked "PLAT" or sometimes with the numbers 950.

## Stones and Gems

Gemstones are formed in nature by a combination of heat, chemicals, and pressure.

Desirable qualities in a stone include beauty, rarity, durability, uniqueness, the ability to reflect light, and, as always, popularity.

Precious stones—rubies, diamonds, emeralds, and sapphires, have rarely gone out of fashion! The long list of semiprecious stones includes topaz, garnet, amethyst, carnelian, peridot, aquamarine, tourmaline, and many others. A number of materials found in nature such as malachite, turquoise, jade, as well as pearls, ivory, enamel, mosaic, and porcelain also can be found in pieces of fine jewelry.

## THE FOUR "C's"

Jewelry experts cite the **"Four C's"—Color, Clarity, Cut, and Carat** as the points to consider when determining the value of a stone.

"Color" has a grading scale of its own, and many of the variances in grade are visible only to the practiced eye.

"Clarity," also sometimes referred to as "purity," measures clearness, referring to the ability of light to pass through a stone without obstruction from flaws or "inclusions" on the inside or outside of the stone.

"Cut" refers both to the shape of the finished stone and to the proportions and faceting, the different elements that have come into play in forming the ready-to-set stone from the rough.

"Carat" refers to the **weight** of a gemstone, not to be confused with "Karat with a K." The weight of a gemstone denotes its size for the purpose of valuation or pricing.

## GRADING AND AUTHENTICITY

The **Gemological Institute of America,** or **GIA,** has a grading system for diamonds that is used throughout the world. The GIA is the world's largest nonprofit educational organization for the jewelry industry. Many jewelers, appraisers, and gemologists have received training from the GIA and retain a professional affiliation with it.

The GIA diamond grading scale has eleven grades for clarity with "Flawless" being the highest, and also evaluates cut, color, and carat weight.

The GIA also sets terms for evaluating colored gemstones, using over thirty-one *hues* to describe color, several measurements for tone and saturation, and fifteen different *clarity types*. You can imagine that there can be literally hundreds of variations of all these elements to arrive at a description of a stone.

A diamond or other stone may be evaluated and graded by a GIA affiliated gemologist, but this is for the purpose of authenticating and determining the quality of the stone, not valuation.

## WHAT THE EXPERT KNOWS

Most jewelers will be able to identify the **metal content** of jewelry, not only from marks, but from small signs of wear, especially at hinges and clasps, color variations, tarnish in silver, and sometimes the weight or "heft" of the piece. If an expert is in doubt, there are ways to **test** metal with chemical solutions and eletronic or digital devices. Both of these can be obtained from jewelry supply stores. The most common testing kit contains a testing stone and three different nitric acid solutions (for 10-, 14-, and 18-karat). Probably this is where the term "acid test" comes from!

**Digital testers** work on a basis similar to metal detectors, interpreting an electrochemical signal. If you have a lot of antique gold jewelry, either unmarked or with rubbed or worn marks, it is not a bad investment. But since there are a considerable number of other factors to evaluate in a piece of valuable jewelry, establishing the metal content may only be the starting point.

**Authenticity of stones** is a more complex science than identification of metals. Even gem experts are sometimes perplexed by a stone. They resort to the resources of a gemological laboratory, where stones can be evaluated with refractive equipment and other tools. Every type of gemstone has its own *refractive properties*, meaning the way it reflects and disperses light. Gemstones have many complex qualities, and the description of a stone prepared by a gemological professional can address many elements, from weight and size, cut, color, hue, tone, and brilliancy, to clarity grades, to analysis of any treatments (called "enhancements") used to intensify or improve the stone.

## IS IT REAL?

There is a lot of "lore" about how to tell if your diamond is authentic, everything from breathing on it to see if it fogs, to viewing it under various types of light. **Cubic Zirconia**, which resembles diamond, has been manufactured since the 1920s and 1930s, as have other synthetic stones. **Moisannite**, a mineral first discovered in meteor fragments and then synthesized as silica carbide, is used today to make imitation diamonds. There are testers for both of these materials, and an experienced eye may notice that moissanite gemstones show double-faceted edges, where diamonds' cut edges are singular in appearance.

You may be able to get some clues as to the authenticity of a stone by looking at other aspects of a piece. Valuable gemstones will rarely be glued down. Any stone with a foil or otherwise colored backing is likely to be inexpensive. Most fine jewelry will use an elongated *prong* or pin that bends over the stone. A flat prong that wraps over the stone might be a clue to an imitation or less valuable type. A finer piece of jewelry is usually designed so that light can reflect through and around the stone, so it is more typically fashioned with openings.

## PEARLS

**Pearls** are made of a material called "nacre." They occur naturally within an oyster, or mollusk, in response to an irritation from a speck of sand or other foreign body.

Pearls can be natural, meaning that they have occurred "spontaneously" inside a mollusk, or cultured. A **cultured pearl** is made by inserting a small bead into the oyster and inducing the production of nacre. The vast majority of pearls sold in the world today are cultured pearls.

The most common strings of pearls are **Japanese Akoya** pearls. The art of culturing round, symmetrical pearls was perfected in Japan by Kokichi Mikimoto, around 1900. Mikimoto acquired some of the first early patents on the pearl-making process. The pearl shop he founded still bears his name and is the leading multinational pearl retailer in the world. Other desirable pearls are from the Australian South Sea and Tahiti.

Pearls are evaluated according first to their *luster*, or bright quality of light. When you see a valuable pearl and notice the almost unearthly way the light emanates from it, you will know this quality again when you see it. Other elements in a pearl's value include size, thickness, transparency, shape, and smoothness. The GIA has no "official" pearl grading standard, but some dealers use descriptions like "AAA" or numerical grades from 1 to 10.

## IS IT REALLY VALUABLE?

What separates the truly important piece of estate jewelry? Jewelry experts agree on a few ingredients:

- It is **signed, stamped, or otherwise proven** to have been made by one of the acknowledged important jewelry designers or manufacturers. **Tiffany, Van Cleef & Arpels, Cartier, Faberge, Bulgari, Boucheron**, and **Schlumberger** are some of the best-known names. A piece of jewelry with a "signature" or manufacturers' mark can be worth several times that of an unsigned but similar piece.
- It contains a **high-quality gemstone** that has been evaluated and ranked in gemological terms. In many cases, it has had its country of origin established. A Cashmere or Burmese sapphire will probably be worth more than one from Thailand or Australia. More and more frequently, major auction houses are selling jewelry with accompanying GIA certification.
- The piece is of a **style or genre** that is currently popular and in demand. An Art Deco diamond clip may sell for many times more than a Victorian brooch. At a 2005 jewelry auction at Doyle's, a ring featuring a pear-shaped **Harry Winston** diamond of 17.22 carats, accompanied by a GIA certificate, sold for $764,000. Other pear-shaped stones in the auction quickly vaulted beyond their estimates. Modern designers such as **David Webb**, who got his start in Hollywood in the 1940s, and **Raymond Yard**, originally jeweler to John D. Rockefeller and other New York scions, are gaining importance.

- The piece has a "**provenance**." It is from the collection of some-one known for accumulating unusually fine pieces, it has a royal or celebrity connection, or it has an otherwise important and documented history.

---

## AT AUCTION

In February 2006, Christie's auctioned the **Graff Ruby**, an 8.62 carat cushion-cut Burmese ruby ring by **Bulgari**, for $3,637,480, setting a new world record per carat for a ruby. A rare, vivid fancy pink diamond ring fetched a record $6.2 million at Sotheby's Hong Kong on April 9, 2006. A two-strand natural pearl necklace broke a world auction record at Christie's Geneva in November 2004, selling for $3,128,520.

---

Apart from the truly prized or sought-after piece, many other fine-quality pieces, both antique and of a more recent vintage, sell regularly at auctions. A jewelry expert on the staff of a local or regional auction company can help you identify a piece that might have a higher degree of marketability, based on his knowledge of what has been in demand.

As with antiques, some design periods are especially popular with collectors and investors. Two of the highest priced antique items in *Warman's Jewelry Field Guide* for 2005 were from the **Art Nouveau** era; a small polychrome enameled **Tiffany** brooch was priced at over $36,000, and contained no precious stones, only a few seed pearls. The Tiffany Studios stamp on the piece was worth more than its weight in gold! An unsigned diamond necklace in the Art Nouveau style, thought to be Russian, was also valued at over $36,000.

Art Deco styles in jewelry lately have been bringing increasingly higher prices.

## FINE JEWELRY VALUES

To determine the value of a piece of fine jewelry or a jewelry collection, you will generally need to enlist the help of a jewelry appraiser or gemologist.

Why? For one thing, gems and jewelry are a specialized area within the appraisal discipline. A gemologist with a lab can authenticate and evaluate stones, look for any signs of enhancement (many gemstones have been heat-treated or irradiated to improve appearance) and detect synthetic or imitation stones. Many jewelry appraisers are **Master Gemologists**, multiskilled professionals with years of experience. They are also familiar with all levels of the jewelry marketplace, and may have training in market research and analysis of pricing.

Supply and demand are factors in jewelry values. Many fine-quality family pieces are of a genre not in short supply. Your appraiser can give you advice on which, if any, stones he feels should be sent to the GIA for evaluation and certification.

## WATCHES

One of the highlights of Sotheby's May 2005 watch sale was a **Patek Philippe single-button split chronograph**, a watch designed to time sporting events such as horse races, manufactured in 1928 for Tiffany's, just prior to the stock market crash of 1929. It was last known to have been sold in New York in 1938. Around 1980, an man in Australia purchased the watch as part of a lot of old items for their weight in gold, then around $25. He had thought it might have some value because of the Tiffany logo on its dial. Later, he opened the watch and found it was manufactured by Patek Philippe.

A somewhat similar Patek "Calatrava" had sold in 1996 for $1.7 million!

The company that became known as **Patek Philippe** began in Geneva in 1939, run by two watchmakers, one an exiled Polish nobleman, Norbert de Patek, and the other a Frenchman, Jean Adrian Philippe. Philippe was the inventor of the stem-winding and hand-setting mechanism that served to modernize wristwatches. Their reputation for high quality and technical innovation rapidly grew, and Queen Victoria of England was an early client. Most of the important developments in watchmaking—self-winding, astronomical dials, chronometers, advanced movements, perpetual calendars—were associated with Patek Philippe. The company still exists today, owned by the Stern family since 1929, and is still considered a premier watchmaker.

Other watch manufacturers emerged: **Rolex** was started in 1908 by Hans Wildorf, a German, who based his company in London and soon became famous for developing the world's first waterproof watch. French master jeweler **Louis-Francois Cartier** created his first watch, called the Santos, in 1904. Leon Breitling started a small workshop in Switzerland in 1894 to manufacture scientific equipment; a few years later his son, Gaston, developed the first wrist chronograph.

**Breguet, Omega, Vacheron and Constantin, Ulysse Nardin, Jaeger-LeCoultre**, and **Movado** are only a few of the many other important watch manufacturers still manufacturing today.

## COLLECTIBLE WATCHES

There are many different kinds of collectible watches; hand-wound watches from the 1920s through the 1950s, automatics, chronometers (precision clocks), calendar watches, and chronographs. Certain watch styles gained popularity or importance through association with a historical event or celebrity, or because the design represented something new.

Ingersoll sold its first **Mickey Mouse watch** in 1933 for $2.75—today it brings over $3000 in good condition. Elvis Presley wore a **Hamilton Electric Ventura** in several scenes of his 1961 movie "Blue Hawaii." Hamilton also pioneered the first digital LED dial, on its **Pulsar** in 1970, which was seen on the wrists of presidents Ford and Nixon, as well as the shah of Iran and other luminaries. In 1969, astronaut Buzz Aldrin walked on the moon wearing an **Omega Speedmaster**, thus insuring this watch's reputation for durability and accuracy. In 1969 a Movado watch dubbed "**Museum**" was added to the Museum of Modern Art's permanent collection in New York.

In 1983 the **Swatch**, an inexpensive plastic sport watch, was introduced in a variety of colors and fashions. The Swatch has rocketed to collectible status lately, with unusual, rare, and artist-designed copies going into the thousands!

The presence of an original band, clasp, and packaging will greatly increase a watch's value.

## COSTUME JEWELRY

Costume jewelry is enjoying a boom among collectors. On any day, you might find fifty thousand different costume jewelry items listed on eBay. Fortunately, because of increasing collector interest, there are many books, identification and price guides, and other materials on the market for costume jewelry. If you should find yourself going through boxes, chests, and drawers of what seems to be inexpensive pieces of jewelry, take heart—there is a growing marketplace for much of it. Information resources also are plentiful, if you have the patience to do a little research and digging.

Some, but by no means all, of the collectible designers and manufacturers include: **Artistic**, **Les Bernard**, **Bliss** (now **Napier**), **Bogoff**, **Marcel Boucher**, **Laura Burch**, **Ciro**, **CIS**, **Coro**, **Miriam Haskell**, **Jonne**, **Joseff**, **Juliana**, **Joseph Mazer**, **Monet**, **Pennino**, **Rebages**, **Renoir**, **Swarovski**, and **Albert Weiss**. Clothing designers such as **Givenchy**, **St. Laurent**, **Schiaparelli**, **Adele Simpson**, **Eisenberg**, and **Hattie Carnegie** also made costume jewelry to go with their clothing.

Costume jewelry is generally made of base metal and either gold or silver electroplate, but sometimes can be sterling silver. You will find a huge variety of materials in costume jewelry including **rhinestone**, **enamel**, **beads**, **marcasite**, **shell**, **mother-of-pearl**, **tortoise shell**, **amber**, **onyx**, **coral**, **jet**, **ivory** and **bone**, **quartz**, and **cameo**. *Bakelite* (pronounced like "bake"), a plastic invented in the early 1900s, was formed into popular bangle bracelets and imaginative pins and brooches in the 1920s and 1930s. **Aurora Borealis** is a glass or sometimes clear plastic that has been coated with an iridescent material to give off a "rainbow" effect.

**Jet**, a hard lightweight black material, which is actually fossilized wood, was popular in the Victorian era and was often made into large carved necklaces and brooches. **Ivory** and **bone** are both materials frequently found in costume jewelry—they can be distinguished from one another by examining the piece under magnification: ivory will have a grain, bone a dotted effect.

The best way to develop an eye for costume jewelry is to see and handle as much of it as you can. Go to shops and to jewelry and vintage fashion shows, examine as many pieces as you can, and ask the dealers questions about them. After a while you will begin to recognize the details of workmanship or special characteristics that make pieces more collectible than others.

## MARKS AND MANUFACTURERS

Many pieces of both fine and costume jewelry are marked with the insignias of their manufacturers. A piece of fine jewelry known to be from a well-known, high quality manufacturer or designer can be worth many times more than an unmarked or unidentifiable piece. **Buccelati**, **Boucheron**, **Bulgari**, **Cartier**, **Faberge**, **Lalique**, **Tiffany**, and **Van Cleef & Arpels** are a few of the most familiar names of jewelry companies that were founded by individual designers in the mid-1800s or early 1900s and still exist today.

## JEWELRY LINGO

Many commonly used jewelry words refer to type and cut of stone or mineral rock, or names of antique pieces (a "sautoir" is a long necklace ending in a tassel; a "chatelain" a small set of household items worn on a chain around the waist). Others are decorative art techniques or descriptive terms.

> Baguette—cut in a narrow rectangular shape
> Blemish—a flaw on the surface of a gemstone
> Briolette—a tear-drop shape with facets
> Cabochon—a rounded stone with a convex shape
> Calibrated—cut to a standard size
> Cameo—shell or stone carved in relief
> Champlevé—enamel placed into carved or sculpted metal
> Enhancement—treatment (heat and irradiation are the most common) to intensify, deepen, or brighten a gemstone
> Emerald Cut—square shaped
> Facet—one of the small plane surfaces made by cutting a stone
> Filigree—thin twisted wire bent into ornamental designs
> Findings—fasteners and construction components used in jewelry making

Gilt—gold plating

Inclusion—technically an internal flaw to the interior of a gemstone, caused by any solid, liquid, or gaseous material. A "fingerprint" of the stone, inclusions can sometimes aid a gemologist in identifying a stone's origin

Intaglio—carving into a stone to create a design

Loupe—magnifying glass

Luster—glow or sheen

Paste—a general term for imitation gemstones

Pave—very tightly set stones, the appearance that the surface of a piece is "paved" with gems

Plique-à-jour—enameled pieces held in delicate metal framing without backing

Vermeil—gold-plated silver

Vitreous—a glassy luster

## FIND OUT ABOUT JEWELRY

The *American Gem Society* website has jewelry education—you can ask for a referral to a jeweler or appraiser there, too. *The Center for Jewelry Studies* sponsors classes and educational events.

Look for a an online costume jewelry portal like *Milky Way Jewels* to compare designs, get cleaning tips, and find links to discussion groups like *The Jewelry Ring*, as well as other jewelry information resource sites like the *Illustrated Dictionary of Jewels*.

*ModernSilver.Com* has a guide to hallmark identification. *Antiquorum* is an auction company devoted solely to watches.

## WHAT TO DO WITH JEWELRY

Costume jewelry and fine jewelry are two different classifications of property, so the first step is to establish which is which.

The first thing to do with any jewelry collection is to separate pieces of value that may need professional evaluation. Look for karat markings, stamps, or hallmarks with a magnifying glass. A mark of "GF" signifies gold filled, "RGP," a mark frequently used in the late 1800s and early

1900s, stands for "rolled gold plating." "HGE" means "hard gold electroplate." "Solid Gold" is an antiquated marking dating from the late 1800, before the 1906 law was passed, and may mean gold filled or rolled gold plate.

## CLUES TO VALUE

Other clues to costume or inexpensive jewelry are: the weight of the piece (costume jewelry may feel lighter), any kind of tarnish or discoloration to gold metal, solid backings, foil or other coating on the backs of stones, flat prongs that seem to hold the stone down rather than out where light can be reflected through it.

Look for any documentation, receipts, previous appraisals, and old jewelry boxes or cases, which may carry a name of a store or manufacturer. Invest in at least one jewelry price guide with photographs, which will help you identify the styles and materials of the things you own.

**Cleaning** jewelry is a subject of some controversy among jewelry experts. Some say you should not clean it by yourself. One thing that is agreed is that no one solution is safe for every piece. There are commercial cleaners for sale at chain stores, which you can test on costume jewelry.

The best and safest thing to use is a polishing cloth, especially for very fine pieces, or a lightly damp rag.

Some silver polishes are too strong for jewelry and will strip the patina from antique silver. You can try a tiny dab of toothpaste to clean up a badly tarnished piece of silver.

## GET THREE OPINIONS

The next step is to get some evaluations of your pieces. Jewelry experts recommend getting several opinions, at least three. Jewelry shows are one place to meet dealers, some of whom may be appraisers and gemologists. Visit a few local jewelers or get a referral from the **American Gem Society** (AGS) until you meet someone you feel comfortable with. You can get a referral to a jewelry appraiser in your area from the American Society of Appraisers website, or any other appraisal organization.

Established auction companies usually have free appraisal clinics. Call to find out when there will be an appraisal day to look at jewelry, or ask about arranging a private meeting.

Many jewelers, like antique dealers, prefer to purchase, rather than consign. Remember that a jewelry dealer will want to buy the piece for 25–30% of what he will sell it for, and sometimes his offer will be less.

Jewelry **brokers** often act as representatives in jewelry sales, taking on the negotiations for you.

You can also try finding an experienced fine jewelry seller on eBay who will work with you as a trading assistant.

## SELLING COSTUME JEWELRY

Costume jewelry is a fun and easy asset that anyone can sell on eBay. Listing and shipping costs are low for small items, and the market of jewelry buyers and sellers is active.

Invest in a **costume jewelry price guide** such as Leigh Leshner's *Vintage Jewelry Price Guide 1920–1940s* or *The Official Price Guide to Costume Jewelry* by Harice Simmons Miller.

Use eBay's discussion boards to post questions, share photos, and get opinions as to the quality, origin, materials, and possible designers of pieces you have not been able to identify. Monitor current and completed items to get an idea of what's selling.

---

*Selling Tip*: Combine inexpensive pieces of costume jewelry into "lots" for sale on eBay—it will sell faster and cost less to ship.

---

If you have enough pieces, jewelry fairs and shows, or antique and collectible fairs that feature jewelry, are also good outlets. You can often rent a "booth" or table space reasonably. Invest in some display cases that you can lock. Visit a few of these events and talk to other dealers about what's selling and get ideas about pricing. Shop until you drop—you can see costume jewelry at antique malls and at vintage clothing shops. The more you see, the more you will educate your eye, and notice familiar qualities in pieces and their prices.

# 8

# RARE COINS AND PRECIOUS METALS

M ost people have a few old coins stashed in a drawer or jar. During the "wild ride" of gold prices in the early 1980s, people invested in coins with reckless abandon. Coins are everywhere, as souvenirs, as pocket change. But how do we know which coins have value?

## COINS IN HISTORY

**Monetary coins** are thought to have originated in ancient Lydia, now a part of Turkey, somewhere around 650–600 BC. Coins were struck by hand until around 1500, when the first mills for punching uniform rounded disks were developed in Italy. During the Renaissance more beautiful and artistic coins were designed. Coins were issued not only by countries and kingdoms, but by cities, duchies, principalities, and other local entities.

Before the Revolutionary War, early U.S. colonists first used British money, but some independent mints were established to strike rudimentary coins, often in the form of tokens. The first American mint was established in 1792, with the production of coins beginning the next year. Coins for the first couple of years were silver. One of the first U.S. gold coins to be struck was the **Brasher Doubloon**, first struck in 1787 by Ephraim Brasher, a friend of George Washington. Only a few have survived, and the rare coin world takes notice whenever one comes up for sale.

---

### AT AUCTION

A group of coin investors paid $2.99 million (the third-highest public price ever for a rare coin) for a **1787 Brasher Doubloon** at a Florida auction held in January 2005.

---

Both gold and silver coins were minted in the United States until 1933, when, at the height of the Great Depression, Franklin Roosevelt ordered all gold coins in the United States removed from circulation and returned to the Treasury. The United States never returned to the "gold standard," and the coins that survived that recall and remained in private hands remain some of the most valuable and sought-after collectible coins on earth.

## BULLION

During the 1980–1981 period, the price of gold skyrocketed to over $800 an ounce. Investors jumped into different kinds of gold, silver, platinum, and coin investments.

**"Bullion" investments** are instruments that *directly track the price of physical gold, silver, and platinum.* Metal bars come in various sizes, starting as low as one ounce, and are convenient for small investors. The first "bullion coin," the **Krugerrand**, was minted in South Africa in 1967, and other similar gold and silver coins began to be minted in countries around the world. **Austrian Coronas**, **Canadian Maple Leafs**, **Chinese Pandas**, and the **American Gold Eagles**, first minted in 1986, are examples of bullion coins. Bullion coins are issued in **sizes** of one ounce and smaller fractions, going down to 1/20th of an ounce.

A bullion coin usually has a "**face value**," such as $50 for an American Gold Eagle, but it is valued at its weight in gold.

Bullion coins are **not considered scarce or rare coins**. Bullion coins and bars, however, have many advantages as an investment. They are easy to identify, buy, and sell. Because gold and silver prices are quoted every day, it is easy to know what they are worth. They have *liquidity*—you can take them into a coin shop or to a precious metals dealer and turn them into cash with relative ease and at low cost. They are convenient to store and are not easily damaged.

## RARE AND COLLECTIBLE COINS

Probably no market for any collectible is as vast as that of rare coins. From teenagers in after-school coin clubs to some of the wealthiest investors in the world, coins have always fascinated. Coins represent wealth and history. People from all walks of life study and collect coins. The volume generated in the rare coin market annually is estimated conservatively to be $2 billion or more!

## TYPES OF COLLECTIBLE COINS

Most collectible coins fall into some basic categories.

**Regular issue or circulated coins** are struck by an authorized government mint for the purpose of legal tender and commercial transactions. Circulated coins make up the vast majority of the rare coin market. Collectors can choose from:

- **Series Coins**—A series collector will accumulate a specific coin in different mintages, such as **Kennedy half dollars, Roosevelt dimes, Jefferson nickels, Lincoln cents**, and so forth.

  Many price guides are organized by series and will list the coins by date, design, and mint marks. Sometimes die variations or very small issuances in certain dates can create a special rarity for a series coin. Earlier series like **Indian Head cents, Barber** (named for the designer) **half dollars**, and **Morgan silver dollars** are examples of some desirable and collectible series.
- **Mint Rarities**—In 1913 a few **Liberty Head nickels** were struck at a time when the mint was transitioning to the Buffalo Head nickel.

A **1913 Liberty Head nickel** sold in 2003 for $2.5 million because of its extreme rarity. Another famous example of a mint rarity is the **1943-S "bronze" Lincoln penny**. Because of World War II, the mint had a shortage of copper and struck most of the 1943 Lincoln pennies in zinc-coated steel. A few scarce pennies, however, were struck on odd copper blanks that still remained in the machines! These rare pennies have sold anywhere from $65,000 to over $200,000.

- **Mis-strikes, mint errors**—Sometimes a coin will be struck off-center, double-struck, or partly clipped off by a machine during the minting process. These odd-looking "mint mistakes" are highly collectible though they may have been discarded at first!
- **U.S. Gold Coins**—because of the 1933 "recall" of U.S. gold coins, the ones that remained in private hands became extremely valuable and represent some of the highest-priced collectible coins on earth. Probably one of the most famous of these is the 1933 **Gold Saint Gaudens Double Eagle**, highly prized for its beauty. Other examples include the **Turban Head Half-Eagle** and **Liberty Head Gold Pieces.** An "eagle" refers generally to a ten dollar gold piece; therefore a "double eagle" has a $20 face amount, a "half-eagle" $5, and so forth. Most gold eagles are worth taking a close look at. Prices can vary quite extensively. One 1907 "high relief" pattern Saint Gaudens type double eagle sold at auction in 2003 for over a million dollars; two other similar 1907 coins were priced in the 2005 *Red Book* at $20,000 and $975 respectively. Differences in the rims, numerals, and edges caused the price variations!

## AT AUCTION

St. Gaudens gold coins are always vaulting to new records. A notable sale took place in July 2002, when an example of the famed **Double Eagle** sold for $7.59 million at an auction conducted jointly by Sotheby's and Stack's. The MS-65 grade from PCGS and the provenance (King Farouk's collection) attracted bidders.

- **U.S. Silver Dollars**—The United States has produced only **nine** silver dollars in history, including the **2000 Sacagawea** coin of today. Many early silver dollars are extremely valuable, particularly the **Draped Bust** (after the portrait on the coin of Lady Liberty, facing right with a garment draped over her shoulder). A rare 1804 **Draped Bust Silver Dollar** sold for more than $4 million dollars at an auction in 1999. As with every coin, variations in grading and other minute details can cause dramatic price differences. On one coin dealer's website recently, one **1878 Morgan Silver Dollar** graded MS 65 was priced at $9700; a very similar coin, also from 1878, but from a different series, graded MS 64, was for sale at only $606.
- **World Coins**—this is a catch-all term for coins produced in other countries besides the United States. Many world gold and silver coins are valuable, but may not have the liquidity or marketability of U.S. coins. You can get a price guide specifically for world coins such as the **Standard Catalog of World Coins** by Chester Krause or the **2005 Black Book Price Guide to World Coins** published by House of Collectibles.

Besides circulated coins there are several other collecting areas of importance:

- **Proof Sets and Mint Sets**—Struck from special proof dies, a proof set is a group of specimen-quality coins with a uniform date. The **U.S. Mint** issues proof sets every year for sale to the public, but not intended for circulation. A proof set will usually have a highly polished, mirror-like surface, and be stored in a protective package. Starting in 1986, the U.S. Mint began to issue certificates of authenticity with proof sets. A **mint set** is a set of coins intended for circulation, struck from regular dies and with regular finish.

  Proof set values are quoted in coin price guides and on some internet coin pricing sites. Except for some rarities, such as sets with missing mint marks, don't be disappointed to find that they are not very valuable. You can find prices quoted in most U.S. coin guides.

- **Commemorative Coins**—Minted to honor a special event, famous person, anniversary, or occasion, these coins are intended for general circulation and are legal tender but are often accumulated by collectors.

  Some commemoratives were issued in rather small numbers; a **Daniel Boone Bicentennial half dollar** from the 1930s might be worth close to $1000, since only two thousand or so were minted in some years. The **1936 Battle of Gettysburg commemorative fifty-cent piece** had a minting of over 26,000, so price guides value that one at only $635, even in MS-65 condition.

  Another type of commemorative coin, sometimes referred to as a **"token" or "medal,"** is commonly issued by a government or private entity to pay tribute to an individual or mark an event, but they are not legal tender. Some have value to collectors but are not really considered coins.

- **Colonial Coins**—Before and shortly after the American Revolution, a variety of coins were used in the early colonies. British, French, and Spanish coins were used because of the economic and trading activities of those three countries. A variety of early tokens and coins was issued by states such as Massachusetts, Vermont, Connecticut, and New Jersey.

- **Ancient Coins**—"Ancients" are coins from approximately **600 BC to 400 AD**, or the start of the Medieval Age. You might imagine because a coin dates from antiquity that it would be more valuable than a modern coin. This is not generally the case in the rare coin market. Ancient coins can be acquired fairly reasonably and are considered a specialized area of coin collecting. Collectors usually focus on a particular period, such as Ancient Greece, or a design or specific theme.

## COIN GRADING

Take a couple of ordinary coins out of your pocket or wallet and look at them closely. Did you ever notice how much wear a nickel or penny has to its surface? Small nicks, marks, and imperfections abound. The surface may be worn almost completely smooth to the point where you have trouble reading the date and letters. On the edge of the coin you may see scratches. The coin itself may not even be symmetrical, one side thinner than the other, or it may even be slightly dented. It may have dirt or grime stuck to it.

Possibly you also have one or two new pennies in your change purse. Notice how the surface of the coin is like a mirror. The copper color is bright and lustrous. The new penny stands out in a group of tarnished, darkened coins that may be only a few years old. Just by comparing the old and new coins you have in the palm of your hand, you are getting your first lesson in **coin grading**.

As we discussed in chapter 3, grading has always been important for coins. The numeric grading scale runs from 1 to 70 with qualifying letters standing for conditions from Poor to Mint State. MS or Mint State grades accompany numbers from 60 to 70. Therefore you might see a coin grading such as: AU (About Uncirculated)-55, or VF (Very Fine)-25.

The use of both letters and numbers gives the grading more "gray scale" to compare very small details of wear and use of the coin. Some of these may not be automatically visible to the naked eye, and may only be seen under light and a magnifying glass!

## PROFESSIONAL GRADING

In the mid-1980s, partly because of the huge boom in coin collecting brought on by the high gold and silver prices of the 1981 period, the coin industry began to adopt a system of **professional or "third-party" grading** for coins. This made it less easy for a coin to be priced based on one person's opinion of its grade. Third-party grading provided a way for collectors and investors to get an independent evaluation of a coin. It is NOT a valuation of the coin, but a qualification of its condition.

When a coin has been professionally graded, it is placed into a protective container, sometimes called a "**slab**." The slab will have an identifying label describing the coin and the grade. It can then be sold by any owner or dealer, or at auction, since it is considered to have been authenticated and evaluated. Third-party grading helped the coin market develop a form of liquidity and marketability not imagined in the past.

Professional grading can cost anywhere from a few dollars to nearly $100 per coin, depending on many factors. For a valuable coin, or a coin that needs authentication, professional grading can greatly improve the chances of realizing maximum value. It is an investment that can protect and enhance the worth of a collection.

## FIND OUT ABOUT RARE COINS

*Coinfacts* is one of the many online encyclopedias of coin information including thousands of images and identification resources. Many coin dealers and auction companies have extensive online sites where you can browse their inventory, search completed sales, and in some cases obtain coin identifications. *Coin Resource* has extensive links to the many **weekly and monthly coin periodicals** that are in print, a reference guide to over seven hundred books on coins, links to coin dealers and grading services, as well as buying and selling services.

The major coin grading services such as *PCGS* **(Professional Coin Grading Service)** and *NGC* **(Numismatic Guaranty Company of America)** have news about coins, coin events, and collector forums.

Most newsstands also carry a selection of coin magazines, and you can find coin price guides at any local bookstore.

## COIN LINGO

There are hundreds of terms used by coin professionals to describe and identify coins. Many of them are names for different kinds of flaws—rubs, spots, abrasions, caused by contact with the coin from some kind of material—a coin bag, a cloth, the minting machinery. Many other coin words are used in grading, and refer to the appearance or condition of the coin. On the PCGS website you can find a glossary with around a thousand examples of coin terminology!

Here are just a few:

Barber—Charles Barber, who designed Liberty Head dimes, quarters, and half dollars from 1892 to 1916 (1915 for the half dollar)
Business Strike—a coin struck for use in circulation

Denomination—face value of a coin

Device—any design element on a coin

Die—steel cylinder with design on it used to strike a coin

Edge—the surface encircling a coin

Error (or mis-strike)—a coin resulting from a mistake in the coining process

Fasces—the symbol of the ax bound in a bundle of sticks on the reverse of the Mercury Head dime struck 1916–1945

Friction—rub or wear on a coin

Hairline—fine, thin, surface scratch caused by wiping a coin with a cloth

Incuse—lettering impressed into a coin (instead of raised)

Legend—words or lettering on a coin

Mercury—dimes minted from 1916 to 1945

Mintage—quantity of a coin made

Mint Mark—small letter or letters on a coin that identify where the coin was struck

Morgan Dollar—U.S. silver dollars made from 1878 to 1921

Planchet—blank piece of metal on which a coin is struck

Press—machinery used to strike coins

Relief—raised portions of a coin such as design elements

Reverse—the back side of a coin

Strike and Struck—striking refers to the process of making coins, and a coin is said to have been "struck" when it is made. The "strike" is also a descriptive term referring to the degree to which metal flows into the recesses of the dies; descriptions of strikes include weak, soft, bold, and full. A coin may also be referred to as "well-struck."

Trime—nickname for a 3-cent silver piece struck from 1851 to 1873

## WHAT TO DO WITH BULLION AND RARE COINS

Finding coins among household belongings is extremely common. You may find what looks like an old jelly jar filled with ordinary change, or a meticulously organized collection in sleeves and slabs. It is rare, though not unheard of, to find a valuable rare coin just sitting around the house, in a drawer or safe. Some people may keep bullion coins this way, with or without identifying documents, but most rare coins of value will be in collections, and it is likely that the collector will have done some work on organizing and cataloging them.

**Bullion coins and bars** are negotiated by gold and silver dealers, and sometimes at banks and brokerage firms. It is easy to check the prices of major bullion coins.

Gold dealers' websites such as **Kitco** have daily quotes on most bullion coins. Some rare coin dealers are also dealers in bullion coins and products.

Values of gold bullion coins and bars should be the same everywhere; they will fluctuate directly with the price of gold. There is a "bid and ask" or differential between the buying and selling price. This can be anywhere from a few dollars for bars to twenty dollars or so for coins. Some dealers will charge an **assay** fee for bullion bars, to weigh and authenticate them if there is any question as to their origin.

---

*Selling Tip*: The sale of bullion is considered a transaction in a financial instrument, and the dealer may require you to fill out a request for taxpayer ID. Bullion may be easier and faster to liquidate than other types of property in an estate so it can be used when there is a necessity to raise cash.

---

With **rare coins**, clues that a collection contains rare or valuable coins are usually that it has been organized, with coins put in albums, or at least stored in plastic "flips" or other types of folders. If any coins have been previously graded, do NOT remove them from their sealed packets.

Don't attempt to **clean** any coins. Coins have been famously damaged by cleaning. In fact King Farouk, whom we mentioned above, was a notorious cleaner of coins, and before investors bid on his St. Gaudens Double Eagle, they had to be reassured by the PCGS graders that the coin had not been cleaned.

Invest in at least **one coin reference book**, such as the *Official Red Book*, which is published annually by Whitman. Even if you know nothing about coins, you can learn from browsing in this guide. By comparing some of the pictures and descriptions to items you may have, you can get an idea quickly if your collection contains desirable items, and some possible clues to the identification of coins you may have.

Rare coins are bought and sold by a wide network of dealers, many of whom conduct auctions. Coin experts recommend that the first step you should take is to get some **bids**, or, offers to buy, on a few of your coins from a variety of dealers. You should get two or three bids on each coin. If you have coins worth over $100, consider having them graded. Graded coins will be easier to sell, and the gradings you receive on the first few may give you an idea of the general condition of the collection.

A large, reputable dealer who conducts public coin auctions is the best bet for selling either a quality collection, or a few valuable pieces. You may have to wait several months to place your coins in a sale. Remember to get several quotes on commissions and fees. Many auction companies will charge between 20 and 30%.

A collection of ancient or world coins may be more difficult to market than U.S. coins, and your best recourse may be to get some offers from local dealers. Try the eBay forums to ask some advice on marketability.

If you find you have a coin collection that is not of great value, not in good condition, or that presents identification problems, give the coins to the younger generation as a gift. It might start some future collector on the path to a rewarding hobby!

# 9

# BOOKS

Books are found in nearly everyone's home. They are so commonplace, not to mention heavy, and cumbersome to pack and move, that they are easily discarded, given away, and donated to libraries and schools on a daily basis. It is easy to give or throw away a valuable book without realizing it!

On the other hand, identifying valuable books can be complex and confusing. True **rare book collecting**, like stamp collecting, is a world filled with minute details, some of which can make a difference of thousands of dollars. It is like a sophisticated mystery game with many rules, some of which seem bewildering at first:

An **old** book is not necessarily more valuable than a newer book.
A book with its **jacket** on it can be worth ten times more than one without.
Not all works by the same author are equally valuable; one book may sell for $2000, another for $1.
Not all first editions are valuable.
An autographed book may be worth less than an unsigned book.
And *a book in fine condition will be worth much more than the same book in lesser condition.*

## USED VERSUS RARE

There are literally millions of used books. Very few of them are actually rare or collectible. Many rare or sought-after books do not *look* different on the surface from the many millions that are only worth perhaps a dollar or so. We know that books provide significant benefits other than monetary— they can be enjoyable to read, or useful for reference and research. But the collector of rare books is after something different: he looks for the scarce, the important, and the pristine.

Book collectors often have special interests. One of the most common is literature. Other specialties include military, medical, historical, scientific, scholarly, or philosophic studies.

---

### AT AUCTION

In 2003, book specialists at Bloomsbury Auctions got a call from a woman who said she had inherited an old Shakespeare book. This copy of the First Folio of *Comedies, Histories and Tragedies* eventually auctioned in April 2004, for close to **$315,000**. The "bargain price" was because the copy was incomplete. Shakespeare's world record was set in 2001, when a First Folio edition of *Hamlet* sold at Christie's for **$6.2 million**.

At Swann's in April 2005, a copy of **Dashiell Hammett**'s *The Glass Key* brought more than four times its original estimate, selling for **$60,000**.

---

Many old books are not rare. Works of famous and popular literature— Dickens, Mark Twain, Poe—have been reprinted countless times. It is rare, but not impossible, to find first editions of major literary works. Jan found a copy of Jack London's *Call of the Wild* among her father's possessions. The copyright page said the book had been published by Macmillan in 1903, and there were two subsequent dates after this, both in 1904.

I researched the book for her at online book retailers. While the 1903 first edition copies of *Call of the Wild* were indeed selling well into the thousands, the second and third printings, from the very next year, were priced around $100. In this lucky case, the book was easy to identify, but many old reprints of popular literary works do not provide as much copyright information as this one.

## RARE BOOK VALUES

What makes a book rare? Very often it has to do with the actual number of copies that were originally printed. If a book becomes popular after its first printing run and has to be reprinted again, the early or **" first" edition** may become a collector's item. A book that had a small printing may not be popular when first published, but if the author then becomes more famous for other works, those scarce early writings soar in value.

In our modern media age, sometimes a **popular movie** can turn an ordinary book into a blockbuster. Norman MacLean was a seventy-year-old retired English professor who had never written a work of fiction before he penned *A River Runs through It* in 1976. The popular movie directed by Robert Redford and starring Brad Pitt made the value of the small first University of Chicago Press printing skyrocket to several thousand dollars. Michael Shaara's *The Killer Angels* enjoyed little commercial success, even though Shaara won a Pulitzer Prize for his 1975 Civil War Novel. Shaara died in 1988 never imagining that his work would later be turned into the hit miniseries *Gettysburg*, and become one of the most collectible books of the 1990s.

Many other writers have been popularized by film, among them Philip Roth, whose early novella, *Goodbye Columbus*, sells for close to a thousand dollars. Raymond Chandler's novel *The Big Sleep* did not bring him instant fame; seven years after it was published, the movie version with Humphrey Bogart finally made Chandler a literary celebrity.

Sometimes a famous book belonging to a famous author, or dedicated by him to someone else, can propel the price into the stratosphere. During the 2004–2005 auction season, a copy of *The Old Man and the Sea* inscribed by Hemingway to Spencer Tracy, who starred in the movie, sold for $310,000.

Other factors can increase value—news, political events, or the death of an author. When John Kerry was running for president during the summer of 2004, signed copies of his book *A Call to Service* skyrocketed to over $300 on eBay and elsewhere. The death of an author can also cause a rise in prices. Copies of Hunter S. Thompson's books such as *Hell's Angels* and *Fear and Loathing in Las Vegas* plus many of his later writings increased in value after his suicide in 2005.

## FIRST EDITIONS

Technically a "first edition" means a copy of a book *printed from the first setting of type*, or the first public appearance of the work in book form. The original typesetting may be corrected, or additional copies printed in response to demand, creating additional "printings" or "states" of the first edition.

So often you will see a book described as "first edition, first printing" or "first edition, first state." With older books, the publishers often did not bother to state that it was the first time the book was printed, or anything else about the printing, except the copyright date. L. Frank Baum's **Wizard of Oz** books, passionately collected today, have been reprinted for virtually a hundred years, but ALL of the reprints issued by Baum's original publisher, Reilly and Lee, through the 1960s bear only the original copyright date.

In more recent years publishers have started to print the words "first edition" on the copyright page, or use a number line such as 1-2-3-4-5-6-7-8-9-10 to indicate a first printing. Without this, **points** or aspects of a book have to be studied to correctly identify first editions.

Points can usually be found on a dust jacket and may include the price of the book, printed on the upper right corner of the inside front flap, other identifying marks such as a photo of the author, or the absence of reviews and accolades present on later copies of the book. On some of Stephen King's first editions there is a number code printed on one of the back pages. Hemingway's publisher, Scribner's, used a letter "A" on the copyright page to denote a first printing. You can find reference books about first editions, and many popular series books such as **Oz, Tarzan, Nancy Drew**, and **Dr. Seuss** have been individually cataloged.

## BOOK CONDITION

As with rare coins, the price of a rare book can vary significantly depending on its condition. As yet, there is no official third-party grading for books.

Most booksellers use a relatively simple scale with just a few general categories. At the top of the scale is "as new," for books in just-published or shrinkwrapped state, not even altered by time on the bookstore shelf. The next category down from the top is "fine," meaning close to new; then "near-fine," "very good," "good," "fair," and "poor."

Most collectors prefer to invest in "near-fine" and above, but "very good" can be a collectible book if it is an antique or something hard to find. Because books suffer many different types of handling wear—small tears, chips to the dust jacket, soiling, loose pages, loose bindings, dirt on the edges, it is important to prepare a detailed description of any book you want to evaluate and get a few different opinions on how it should be graded.

## DO YOU HAVE COLLECTIBLE BOOKS?

Major categories of more modern collectible books include:

- **Modern American Literature and Fiction**—important writers such as **Faulkner**, **Hemingway**, and **Steinbeck**; other novels from the 1950s and 1960s that are in demand include **Harper Lee**'s *To Kill a Mockingbird*, **Jack Kerouac**'s *On the Road*, **J. D. Salinger**'s *The Catcher in the Rye*, **Ayn Rand**'s *The Fountainhead* and *Atlas Shrugged*—all of which have sold in the $5–10,000 range recently in fine condition. Titles such as **Joseph Heller**'s *Catch 22* and **Ken Kesey**'s *One Flew over the Cuckoo's Next* are not far behind, both in the $3000 range in recent sales.
- **Hot Modern Firsts**—first books by successful best-selling authors, such as **John Grisham**'s *A Time To Kill*, which sells for over $1000 in fine condition. Fine copies of Stephen King's first few titles, *Salem's Lot*, *The Shining*, and *Carrie*, have climbed into the midhundreds, as have **Anne Rice**'s early Vampire titles. Other favorites increasing in value have been Kurt Vonnegut, Dean Koontz, Ian Fleming's James Bond series (British editions, please!), and Larry McMurtry (movies again).
- **Children's Books**—Popular vintage children's series books include **Winnie the Pooh, The Black Stallion, Nancy Drew and Hardy Boys mysteries, Tom Swift, Beatrix Potter,** and **Little House on**

the Prairie. **Harry Potter** has started to give the older book series a run for their money lately.

Early **Walt Disney** studio books, and **Dick and Jane** readers from the 1940s (*yes, really!*) have also been increasing in value.

- **Science Fiction and Fantasy**—**Philip Dick, Robert Heinlein**, early **Asimov, L. Ron Hubbard, Frank Herbert, Tolkein**'s *Lord of the Rings*
- **Fine Bindings**—(including leather and slipcased editions)
- **Westerns and Americana**—including early books about fishing and other sports
- **Mysteries**—**Dashiell Hammett** is most revered, also **Raymond Chandler, Ellery Queen**, early **Agatha Christie**
- **Art Books**—issued in limited quantity or that contain original art work
- **Historical and Scholarly Texts**—often sought after by libraries and historical societies

**Bibles** are commonly found in home libraries; most have only sentimental value, but a few are collectible if they have rare bindings or historical significance.

Most **paperbacks** are not valuable, but it is still possible to uncover a gem or two among them. *Pulp mysteries* from the 1930s are very desirable, as well as many scarce early science fiction titles. Lately some "vintage" **Jack Kerouac** copies such as early paperback editions of *On the Road* have started to increase in value. Poetry and other literary items (**Charles Bukowski, William Burroughs**) from the Beat period and early 1960s issued by small presses in limited paperback editions are also starting to gain interest. Softcovers from **TV series** and **Star Wars** are collectible in sets.

## WHAT THE EXPERT KNOWS

The book expert has an excellent memory for details. He might be a collector, a dealer, an academic scholar or archivist, a historian, a librarian or researcher, possibly a writer of books about books, or a professor of literature who collects as a hobby. You may find him on the staff of some specialized auction houses such as Swann's or Bloomsbury.

He will be able to tell a good deal about the age of any book from the weight and appearance of the paper, and details of the binding. He *may* be a human encyclopedia of first edition points, but if not, he has a library to look them up in. Additionally, he may be familiar with obscure authors, early manuscripts, even printing and binding techniques.

## BOOK LINGO

Antiquarian—loose term referring to collectible books, NOT the same meaning as "antique"

Boards—cloth book covers

Calf—leather binding

Colophon—identifying inscription, as an emblem or lines of text containing printing information

Copyright Page—the page, usually just before or after the title page, that tells the date the book was published and sometimes states the edition

Dust Jacket or Dust Wrapper—paper book cover

Endpapers—the first and last pages of a book including the pages pasted to the covers.

Flyleaf—a blank page at the front of the book

Laid In—inserted in the book but not attached, such as a note, card, or other information

Pastedown—attached to a cover, such as an endpaper or a printed illustration on a cover

Tipped-In—partially attached

Vellum—thin sheet of calf, lamb, or kidskin used for covers

Wraps—outer covers of a paperback book

## FIND OUT ABOUT RARE BOOKS

On the *Smithsonian Library*'s website there is a list of recommended resources for book collectors, among them the *OCLC (Online Computer Library Center)* at **www.oclc.org**.

There is also *The American Library Association's Rare Books and Manuscript Section*, which has links to extensive resources for archivists and librarians. ***Rare Books Info*** has research bibliography material as well as an archive of auction results.

You can usually locate a rare book scholar or expert at a university library or a museum or historical society, and ask for advice on using the online bibliographies. The Smithsonian also recommends price guides such as Allen and Patricia Ahearn's ***Collected Books*** (updated every few years), which you can purchase, and **American Book Prices Current**, an index that sells for over $50—you can find it at a local library.

You can also run a search on a number of free book websites such as ***Faded Giant*** or use the inventory on large book-selling sites such as ***Advanced Book Exchange*** to research prices, get descriptions, and contact rare book dealers to ask questions. The eBay forums are frequented by some knowledgeable book enthusiasts who can answer questions and look at digital photos you provide.

## WHAT TO DO WITH BOOKS

Separate your books into categories such as fiction, history, geography, children's.

What do you know about the person who owned the books?

What about the way in which the books were acquired? Do any of the books have inscriptions or dates written in them? Are there any materials inside them? Notes, receipts, news articles, even a birthday card or letter can give clues to the age of a book. Do any of them have bookstore stamps or stickers?

Knowledge you have about how and where books were acquired will help you date them when the copyright pages don't provide enough details.

## SELLING BOOKS

Dealers and collectors scour eBay for treasures. If you've tried to research a book and can't figure out what printing it is or whether it's valuable, you can just try listing it, describing everything about it, with photos, and see what kind of bids you receive.

If you feel you have books that might be valuable, you can have them evaluated by a rare book dealer or by an expert at an auction company. Most major and regional auction houses are staffed with book and manuscript specialists. *Swann's*, *Pacific Book Auctions*, and *Bloomsbury* in London are a few auction companies that specialize in books and other printed matter.

EBay is an active marketplace for booksellers and buyers. You can consult with a trading assistant who specializes in books to get an opinion on how well your books may sell. If you check completed listings over a period of time, you'll get an idea what is selling, and you may decide to try your luck.

---

*Selling Tip*: *Brodart* sells protective mylar wrappers for book jackets, which will safeguard paper covers, as well as make your books look professional.

---

If you meet with a local rare book dealer, she will probably want to purchase books outright from you, but the knowledge you gather about their potential value will help you negotiate with her. Book fairs are an excellent way to meet and talk with dealers.

In the case of a collection that may contain only one or two truly valuable books and many lesser ones, you may actually be better off accepting a package offer from a dealer.

Used books that are not rare or collectible can be sold or traded at used bookstores or yard sales, or donated to libraries. Some organizations accept donations of books for military personnel stationed overseas, and many diverse foundations support reading programs and aid and outreach with books. Hospitals, schools, shelters, and a variety of other charities also welcome books as donations. Check with your library to see when they are having a book drive; some libraries have sales during the holidays and welcome donations in gift condition.

# 10

# DOLLS AND TOYS

For Christmas in 1964, Rusty's grandfather gave him a new doll that had been created especially for boys, GI Joe dressed as a soldier.

Rusty, who was four, also received a stuffed rabbit and a gardening set with real seeds and a little shovel, trowel, and pail. He immediately bonded with his new rabbit, and took it outside with him despite the ice on the ground to try his hand at gardening. He showed little interest in GI Joe, looking at it once, and putting the box carefully back under the Christmas tree with some of his other gifts.

"Aren't you too big for a stuffed bunny?" Rusty's father Al joked. "Look at this terrific soldier doll your Grandpa got you. Did you see he has a gun?"

Rusty's mother Jean took the box from Al, frowning slightly.

"He doesn't like the soldier. I don't want him to play with a violent toy. He loves animals and flowers, can't you see?"

Jean nodded at her son, who was curled in a chair with his bunny, the gardening tools close by him on the floor, showing him pictures in a book of birds and flowers.

"Maybe we can return the soldier to the toy store and exchange it for another animal," suggested Al. Keep it in the package and put it in the closet. I'll find out what store Dad bought it from."

"Good idea." Jean took GI Joe from beneath the tree and placed the package carefully on an upper shelf in the hall closet. Rusty never asked to see it, and Jean was just as glad.

Shortly after Christmas Rusty's grandfather suffered a stroke, and in the flurry of hospital visits that followed, GI Joe was quickly forgotten. Winter coats and hats filled the closet in spring, and it was several years later when Jean found the boxed toy during spring cleaning and transferred it to a box in the basement along with some of Rusty's other toys and clothing that had been outgrown.

Years passed. Rusty went to college, majoring in biology. Eventually he became a professor and was married with two young sons, Zack and Steven. The boys were as different as night and day, Zack athletic and outgoing, captain of the swim team. Steven was quiet and reserved. He liked books and web-surfing. He was curious about history and many other topics. Rusty worried sometimes that Steven was too introverted, but he wasn't sure how to approach his son about it.

One morning at breakfast Rusty told his sons that Al and Jean had sold their home and were moving to a retirement community.

"I'd like you two to help out on Saturday. Grandma has some boxes of things she wants us to pack and take over to the Salvation Army."

"Dad, I've got swim practice," Zack protested. "It's the last before the State Finals."

"It's okay, I can help you, Dad," Steven put in. He liked his grandparents and would be sorry not to make any future visits to their home.

On Saturday Steven found himself in the basement of Al and Jean's home, packing some old curtains and sheets into cartons. An unsealed box against one wall caught his eye; on it his grandmother had written "Rusty" in large letters with a black marking pen. Curiosity got the better of Steven, and he pulled back one corner to peek under the carton. Inside were children's books, some earlier versions of ones he himself had read, clothes, records, stuffed animals, games, and other toys. Steven examined some of the items. It was interesting to imagine his father as a little boy playing with these things. At the bottom of the carton his hand brushed a carton, he looked down and saw the GI Joe doll, untouched and still in its original package.

"How are you doing?" Jean asked suddenly, startling him. Steven had not heard his grandmother coming down the steps and he drew in his breath in excitement.

"Grandma—where did you get this GI Joe?"

Jean reached over and took out the box, laughing.

"Oh, my gracious. I had forgotten we still had this toy! Al's father, your dad's Grandpa, gave that to your father one Christmas. I didn't have the heart to tell him Rusty wasn't interested in soldiers. He never played with it, and we were going to return it and just forgot."

"Grandma, this is valuable. Did you know that? This is an original. It's still in the box. It's a collector's item!"

Jean was pleased to see Steven so enthusiastic about something.

"Well it certainly is no use to us where we're going, so if you'd like to keep it, it's yours." Rusty was astounded to see his son so animated when he heard about GI Joe. He was surprised to learn Steven knew the history and value of other collectible toys as well, including Star Wars and other action figures.

Steven kept GI Joe in the box on the desk in his room and continued his interest in toys. He visited thrift shops and garage sales looking for valuable items. He eventually launched an informational website for collectors, wrote an article for the local paper, and won an award at school for restoring an antique model train he had found. He was more confident and outgoing, and achieved popularity equal to his brother's.

"You know, Dad," he told his father one day, "that GI Joe is not even as valuable as I had thought when I first saw it. Some of the models that came after the first series actually bring higher prices."

"Really?" Rusty kept his true thoughts to himself. In his opinion, GI Joe was priceless!

Steven knew something that a lot of us might not: toys are one of the largest and most dynamic collector markets today. From Darth Vader to Dinky cars, many of the toys we played with and bought for our own children have become valuable. Grading has begun to be important for toys, and the rarest of items never removed from boxes or wrappings command the highest prices.

## DOLLS

Long before the concept of movie heroes and comic book characters come to life, dolls were enjoyed by children as well as by devoted collectors. The doll collecting community is large and well organized, with a large national parent club, the *United Federation of Doll Clubs* (*UFDC*) and several major regular magazines. Dolls have a relationship to history, costume design, nostalgia, art, antiques, and entertainment, as they sometimes represent movie characters and celebrities. Many dolls both antique and modern are elegant, one-of-a-kind masterpieces of craftsmanship and detail.

Valuable and collectible dolls fall into three "periods":

### Early Dolls—Pre-1920

Dolls have been found that date from as far back as the 1500s—early dolls were often made of paper, papier mâché, cardboard, or wood. Most of these examples today are found in museums. Around the 1700s, cardboard dolls were used as mannequins to display fashions and the concept of the "paper doll" was born.

Some of the most valuable collectible dolls have heads made of **bisque (unglazed porcelain), china, celluloid, or wax**. Early doll bodies were made of materials like rags, wood pulp, or sawdust—material referred to generally as "**composition**."

France and Germany were the leading doll manufacturers of the 1800s, when dolls became more popular as children's toys. By far one of the most important French manufacturers of dolls was **Bru Jne. & Cie**, which began making dolls in 1866 and continued through 1899. Bru dolls regularly sell for upwards of $10,000, with some reaching into the $30–40,000 range! Even the head of a Bru doll or a doll with flaws or restoration can be valuable. The Bru is so sought after that like other antique dolls it has been extensively reproduced by modern doll companies, such as **Hamilton**. You may see these dolls referred to as "antique reproduction dolls," and they may command prices in the high hundreds or even low thousands. **Emile Jumeau** was another early French doll manufacturer of the mid- to late 1800s who specialized in the bisque **Bebe** doll among others.

Bru dolls and others can be identified by marks on their heads. Often a numerical sequence of one to four digits will signify a mold or the size of the doll, or both. Other manufacturers' marks on dolls may include initials, symbols, and names.

Other German and French dolls vary in price with marked pieces from manufacturers such as **Kestner, Dressel, Simon and Halbig, and Klammer and Reinhardt** bringing higher prices than dolls of unknown makers. **Kathy Kruse** was a pioneer in German doll making of the early twentieth century. She disliked the hard look of bisque and used painted pressed cloth for her expressive faces. **Gabriel Heubech and Armand Marseille** were an important German doll maker who manufactured lovely dolls from the late 1800s well into the 1920s. Other makers of this era include **Goegel, Henrich Handwerck, Schmidt, Walther & Sohn, Saltier, Steiner**, and **Bahr**.

---

### AT AUCTION

Therriault's April 2005 Las Vegas auction featured a 1915 portrait artist doll by the French sculptor **Albert Marque**, which sold for $175,000. A rare 18-inch **Bru Bebe Modele** with a wooden body soared past its presale estimate of $12–15,000, selling for $42,000. The dolls in the sale were from the collection of Mildred Seeley, a noted doll researcher and author.

---

Early American doll making was slow to develop. At first American dolls used French or German heads. The bisque **Kewpie** doll, introduced in 1912, based on illustrations in *The Ladies' Home Journal* by artist Rose O'Neill, was the first important American doll, and it was an instant hit, as popular in its day as Barbie and Cabbage Patch would become in theirs.

The first Kewpies were made in Germany by **J. D. Kestner** for **George Borgfeldt** of New York, which became one of the first major American doll companies. Despite its historical importance, prices of Kewpies, unless exceptionally rare or unusual, have remained fairly low. The **Rose O'Neill** bisque Kewpies from 1912 to 1920 have the best value but routinely sell in the hundreds.

**Raggedy Ann,** based on the Johnny Gruelle cartoon illustrations, appeared in 1918. The first dolls were sold by **P. F. Volland,** the books' publisher, until 1934, when they were licensed by **Georgene Averill.** Early Volland dolls have sold for well into the thousands.

## "Middle Period" Dolls—1920s through 1960s

High-quality bisque was finally manufactured in the United States around 1918. World War I depressed European doll production, and by the early 1920s the United States had become a leading doll manufacturer. Technological innovations through World War II included latex rubber and plastic vinyl, making dolls easier to form and less expensive.

**American Character,** founded in New York in 1918, was one of the early American success stories. **Georgene Averill,** who received an early "mama doll" patent in 1918, created signature dolls with lifelike faces and pudgy "apple" cheeks, as well as cloth dolls. In 1923 a fledgling doll company was launched in New York by Beatrice Alexander. Alexander's family had a long history in dolls and costuming. **"Madame" Beatrice Alexander** strove to produce high-quality dolls, starting with nurse and baby dolls, then expanding to famous characters from books and history (Alice in Wonderland, Queen Elizabeth, the girls of *Little Women*). Madame Alexander was famous for bride and bridesmaid dolls in luxurious, detailed gowns in the 1950s, and dominated the world of dolls through the late 1960s.

Other collectible doll makers from this period include **Effanbee, Arranbee, Ideal** (famous for **Betsy McCall**), **Nancy Ann,** and the **Vogue** Doll Company of Massachusetts, which introduced its **"Ginny"** doll in 1948. Ginny was the first modern collectible doll whose clothes could be purchased separately. She was sold in many costumes and versions, starting a tradition that would be carried on by the groundbreaking emergence of **Mattel's Barbie** in 1959.

Barbie was an instant celebrity. With an adult body, designer wardrobe, supermodern hairstyles, and accessories galore, Barbie involved children and preteens in a world of sophistication and allure. She epitomized the glamour of the fast-paced 1960s, and was produced in a variety of styles until the early 1970s, when quality declined and Barbie's fad began to ebb. In the

1990s, Mattel reintroduced Barbie as a collectible doll, some in porcelain and others in elegant gowns designed by Bob Mackie.

Prices of the earliest Barbies average in the hundreds, although the record sale for a **"#1 blonde ponytail Barbie"** (mint condition) is $25,500!

**Cabbage Patch Kids**, conceived by Xavier Roberts and licensed by Coleco, was a doll success story that began in 1983. The soft dolls had endearing, lumpy faces and all came with "birth certificates" and "adoption papers." For the first few years, demand for the dolls exploded, and Coleco's sales topped $600 million by 1985. Cabbage Patch dolls have been relicensed several times and are still made today, but some rarer 1980s originals can sometimes sell in the $100–300 range.

## Modern Art and Collector Dolls

Doll collecting enjoyed a resurgence in the 1990s and many exquisite dolls are being fashioned today in a variety of price ranges. There are several basic types of modern collectible dolls: *one of a kind, artist limited editions*, and *manufactured limited editions*.

**Ashton Drake**, the **Franklin Mint**, and the **Danbury Mint** produce modern collectible dolls in the $1–300 range with several models, those of Marilyn Monroe, Princess Di, the Wizard of Oz characters, and Jacqueline Kennedy being the most popular in the resale market. Many other modern dolls are artistic reproductions of famous dolls, and some lines, such as Kathy Kruse, are still owned by family descendents who manufacture dolls in the original style and tradition.

**Robert Tonner** is a former leading fashion designer who revived the classic 1950s Betsy McCall doll (originally made by American Character) and developed the stylish, sophisticated **Tyler Wentworth** and **Sidney Chase** dolls. Madame Alexander has the modern fashion doll **"Alex"** in this category as well.

**R. John Wright**, who works in upstate New York, has revived Raggedy Ann and other storybook characters such as Winnie-the-Pooh. Other modern, original doll artists include **Helen Kish, Susan Wakeen, Audrey Swarz, Jan McLean, Wendy Lawton, Annette Himstedt**, and **Hildegard Gunzel**, known for her evocative, lifelike faces.

Older dolls in good condition can be difficult to find, for obvious reasons. Typical flaws to dolls include dirt, chips, cracks, scratches, missing eyes and other parts, mold, insect damage, loose limbs, torn or missing costumes, and general wear and tear from being played with. The presence of an original box, package, stand, or tag will greatly enhance the value of any vintage or collectible doll.

Because of the proliferation of reproduction dolls, it can be important to get dolls evaluated by a knowledgeable expert. Visit a doll convention or toy fair to meet and chat with dealers. *The National Association of Antique Doll Dealers* has a membership directory you can access online, or check with the *UFDC*.

## TEDDY BEARS

The Teddy Bear is the most collectible stuffed animal and a close cousin of the doll. There are several different stories about who might have invented the first Teddy Bear. The **Steiff** company started as a felt garment manufacturer in Germany during the 1800s. In 1880, **Margarete Steiff** fashioned a pin cushion in the shape of an elephant, and the first stuffed animal may have been born. By the 1890s, Steiff was manufacturing many different animals; Margarete had secured patents on her toys and had introduced a catalog.

Richard Steiff, Margarete's nephew, an artist and toy designer who spent time sketching zoo animals, is said to have seen performing bears in a circus on a visit to America around 1900, and got the idea for a bear that could move its arms, legs, and head. The first Steiff teddy bear was introduced in Leipzig at the 1903 Spring Toy Fair and over twelve thousand bears were sold at the 1903 World's Exposition in Saint Louis. The Teddy Bear has been the most successful stuffed animal in toy history ever since.

Around the same time in the United States, a famous cartoon circulated in the newspapers about President Theodore Roosevelt and a cub he encountered on a bear hunting trip. Roosevelt's aides had procured the cub as an easy target for the president, who had failed to hunt down a trophy bear, and Roosevelt refused to shoot the defenseless cub. At their New York candy store, **Rose** and **Morris Michtom** got the idea to sew a plush velvet bear with shoe button eyes to sell with their notions and other penny items. They called it "**Teddy's Bear**," and when it was an instant hit, they sent a copy to the president, who gave them permission to use his name for the bear.

Demand for the bears was so great that the Michtoms started making them full time, and their factory grew into the **Ideal Toy Company**. The original plush bear they sent to Roosevelt is now in the Smithsonian Institution. Although the Michtoms tried and failed to get a patent for the Teddy Bear, they were granted a license to produce Smokey the Bear teddies in 1953.

Other companies developed in Germany and also in England, including **Merrythought** and **Chad Valley**, who obtained a British Royal Warrant of Appointment, and through its merger with **Chiltern** became the largest stuffed animal manufacturer in England in the 1960s.

Steiff is considered the "top of the line" when it comes to bears and animals. Most famous Teddy Bear sales have been of Steiff bears. A black Steiff made in 1912 to commemorate the sinking of the Titanic sold at Christie's in 2000 for $136,000. Another notable price in 1994 was 110,000 British Pounds for "Teddy Girl," a 1904 Steiff that belonged to Colonel "Bob" Henderson, a collector and founder of the Teddy Bear Club and Good Bears of the World, which donated bears to childrens' charities.

Steiff bears can be identified by a *trademark nickel or brass button* in one of their ears. A tag and sometimes a woven label were also usually present. Early Steiff bears can easily bring from $2000 to $6–7000 at auction or from dealers, and tend to bring competitive prices on eBay as well.

Another popular German bear was the "yes-no" bear introduced in 1921 by **Schuco**, whose head could be moved up and down or side to side by a lever in its tail. A "yes-no" bear from the 1950s sold recently for $1,200 on eBay—earlier models can fetch in the mid-thousands. Many other vintage bears sell routinely in the mid-hundreds.

## WHAT THE EXPERT KNOWS

A doll expert will closely study the materials in the doll, especially details such as eyes, hair, and eyelashes, and the face and details of the costume. The valuable doll's face should be clean and free of blemishes, and the costume and shoes should be original, not repaired or altered. She or he will look for manufacturer marks, serial numbers and tags, and will be familiar with many of the models produced by specific manufacturers at different times. The teddy bear afficionado will look for tags and the characteristic Steiff button, but will also know the materials used to make feet and eyes, and the different styles, colors, and types of wool that were used by various manufacturers at different times.

Some people say that the smell of an old Teddy Bear is unmistakeable— but since many bears were stored away in attics and boxes with other old things, this technique may not be reliable!

## ACTION FIGURES

GI Joe, introduced by Hasbro in 1964, was the first male doll. An early vision by **Hasbro** CEO Merrill Hassenfeld, Joe predated the modern-day action figure by twenty years, and would eventually spawn a multi-billion-dollar market that thrives in the high-tech, multimedia entertainment world of today.

There were four early GI Joes similar to Rusty's Christmas gift in realistic military garb representing Soldier, Sailor, Pilot, and Marine. The toy's popularity soared until 1968, when opposition to the Vietnam War catalyzed a change in the doll from a military soldier to an outdoor adventurer. By 1969, Joe had appeared as Frogman, Diver, Astronaut, Adventurer, and several other modes complete with costumes and accessories.

The Adventure Series was popular until the 1970s, when costs began to rise, and Joe's popularity finally began to wane, but before temporarily going out of production in the late 1970s, Joe had become a defender of safety in the universe, outfitted with vehicles, weapons, and a command center.

In the 1980s Star Wars era, Hasbro reintroduced Joe in a smaller, 3 3/4-inch format as an action figure fighting "evil forces." By 1994, Joe was back in his original 12-inch size, and lines such as Classic Collections continue to be produced today.

Soon after Joe's introduction and meteoric success in the 1960s, competitors such as the **Louis Marx** company began manufacturing military action dolls and soon expanded to a line of heroes of the Old West such as **Daniel Boone** and **Davy Crockett**. The Marx line included characters from western TV shows such as *Bonanza* and *Wild Wild West*. **Ideal** was another important action figure manufacturer in the 1960s, introducing the "**Captain Action**" figure who could be transformed from one character to another by a change of costume! Captain Action figures from this period command some of the highest prices for vintage action toys today.

In the early 1970s, manufacturers such as **Mego** jumped into the act, with **American West**, early **Star Trek, World's Greatest Super Heroes, Flash Gordon**, and **Action Jackson** dolls among others. In 1977, the first **Star Wars** movie was released. Kenner received the license for the rights to toys and games, and introduced the 3 1/2-inch action figure. By the early 1980s the action figure market was going full throttle; Mattel brought out **Masters of the Universe** and **Marvel Super-Heroes, Coleco** licensed **Rambo**, Kenner introduced **Transformers. Dungeons and Dragons** and **Dr. Who** were also popular figures of the late 1980s. The 1990s brought the **Mighty Morphin Power Rangers** from **Bandai, Spawn** from **MacFarlane, Spider-Man** from **Toy Biz**, later Star Trek figures from **Playmates**, and an updated Batman line from **Kenner**.

## ACTION FIGURE VALUES

There are literally thousands of collectible action figure toys ranging in price from just a few dollars to thousands. The **classic GI Joes** similar to the one that Steven found Mint in Box sell in the midhundreds, while the Canadian Mountie, Military Police, Shore Patrol, and other specialty lines from the later 1960s with full equipment in boxes, have sold for more than $3000. The 1960s **Captain Action dolls from Ideal** rule the roost with prices in the $2–4000 range.

Grading is becoming more prevelant for action toys. The *Action Figure Authority* **(AFA)** is a company that has recently begun grading action figures and pricing graded toys.

## EARLY CAST-IRON VEHICLES

Some of the highest priced items in the toy universe are from the turn of the century, when manufacturers such as **Arcade, Wilkins, Carpenter, Ives, Hubley, Kenton**, and **AC Williams** turned out early cast-iron replicas of farm equipment, railroads, horse-drawn wagons, fire-fighting vehicles, and military caissons. Some of the early makers, like Kenton, were in the hardware or lock and key business, and made their first toys for promotional displays.

---

## AT AUCTION

A rare, intricate **Carpenter "Tally Ho" coach** drawn by four horses rocketed to a record $92,200 at James D. Julia's February 2005 toy sale. At the same sale a **Carpenter** replica of a burning brownstone sold to a toy museum for $54,625, and a **Pratt & Letchworth** horse-drawn military caisson fetched $60,375.

---

Many other unique cast-iron toy objects from the early 1900s are in demand, including mechanical banks, bell toys, doorstops, carousels, and cap guns.

## MODEL VEHICLES

Possibly no collectible market is as huge as model vehicles. Any day on Google, there are over one million results for the search word "Diecast." On eBay there are over one hundred thousand listings every day, making toy vehicles one of the highest-volume categories. American men and boys (and no doubt girls!) have had a love affair with model cars and trucks since around the time that real-life autos first appeared.

**Buddy L** was one of the first important manufacturers of toy cars. Buddy L was started by **Fred Lundhal**, founder of the Moline Pressed Steel Company, which made parts for International Harvester and Deering. Lundhal made a toy truck for his son Arthur (nicknamed "Buddy") reportedly out of some scrap metal. Other kids in the neighborhood clamored for trucks of their own, and Lundhal decided to experiment with his models at the 1922 New York Toy Fair. Sales at first were not spectacular, but by 1923 the model trucks and cars had taken off, and Lundhal abandoned his "grown-up" auto parts business and turned full time to the world of toys. By 1926 many different models were being produced, among them fire engines, vans, tanker trucks, tugboats, buses, airplanes, and trains. These highly detailed 1920s toys are considered some of the most valuable collectible model vehicles in existence. In fact a Buddy L **"Red Baby"** truck with enclosed cab sold for $22,000 at a 1995 auction, and a two-door model shattered records at $28,600 three years later!

**Dinky Toys**, first called Modelled Miniatures, came on the market in 1933, made by a British manufacturer known for electric trains. They were manufactured in both Britain and France, and used numbers to identify models. **Marx Toys**, already a producer of model trains, also started manufacturing toy cars in the 1930s, and included cartoon character vehicles in their line.

By the 1950s the toy car market was getting flashier, more sophisticated, and diverse. **Corgi**, **Ertl** (famous for John Deere Tractor models), **Exoto**, **Matchbox**, **Dugu**, **Tonka**, **Lincoln**, **Structo**, and **Tootsie** are a few of the desirable brands prominent in the 1950s and early 1960s.

In 1968 **Mattel** introduced its first eighteen **Hot Wheels** models, revolutionizing the world of collectible cars. Hot Wheels were sleek, stylish, well detailed, and fast moving, and were made in a variety of racing styles. Like the markets for dolls and action figures, model cars enjoyed a renaissance in the 1980s and 1990s. Names like **Bburago**, **Brookfield**, the **Danbury Mint**, and **Nascar** also figure prominently in today's market.

The **Toy Cars Collectors Association** lists 962 manufacturers of diecast and other metal model cars on their website. Mint condition examples of early vintage toy cars can range from the low-to-mid-hundreds into the thousands. Fortunately, it's a market with extensive web resources and collectors' guides.

## MODEL CAR VALUES

Prices of diecast cars can range anywhere from a few dollars to many thousands. In Karen O'Brien's guide, the top ten prices, ranging from $5000 to $11,500, were for **Buddy L** vehicles from the 1929–1932 period, and several scarce **Johnny Lightning Topper** 1960s Mustangs, Camaros, T-Birds, and Chargers, which were priced at $6000. Topper produced the original cars briefly in the late 1960s to compete with Hot Wheels, and the line has been recently revived.

On an ordinary day on eBay, I saw a vintage 13-inch **Kingsbury** tow truck sell for $4375, a 1950s **Tonka** delivery truck with rust spots for $2325, and a 1973 **Matchbox** Duesenberg with box for $2154. A 1971 hot pink

Porsche 917 from the **Hot Wheels Redline** line was selling for over $50; a sixty-one-piece lot of Redline models from the 1960s sold for $1826.

Remember, though, that for every four-figure sale in model vehicles, there are hundreds if not thousands of low priced cars as well. In O'Brien's guide, a 1970 Buddy L Brute Super Bug VW Beetle is worth just $8, even Mint in Box, and a 1960s Hot Rod Woody Station Wagon, made in Japan, is priced at $35. Modern diecast cars are plentiful, so supply factors are important in the pricing of all but the rarest models.

## MODEL TRAINS

Model railroads may not have blossomed in the internet age in the same way as action figures and toy cars, but they do still have their enthusiasts. Recently a 773-1950 **Lionel Hudson** engine (with original box) sold on eBay for $6100. The original **Lionel** company was founded in New York in 1900 by Joshua Lionel Cowan and Harry C. Grant. Their original intention was not to make toys. The first model train, which used a battery and electric fan motor, was part of a store window display, designed just to attract attention. Instead, people began asking if the trains were for sale. Model trains had been made in Germany by a company called **Marklin** a decade or so earlier. Other early makers included **Bing** in Germany, **Ives** in the United States, and **Hornby** in Britain.

Hornby was named after its founder, Frank Hornby, who invented and patented a children's toy model-making kit which could be disassembled, the parts used in different models. In 1907, Hornby established a parent company, **Meccano**, which was an innovator in all types of toys through the 1960s.

## OTHER ANTIQUE TOYS

Many types of vintage and antique toys are collectible. Some of the more interesting categories include:

> Lead Soldiers: **Britains**, founded in 1845, usually command the highest prices, especially for sets in original boxes; **Barclays**, **Charbens**, and **John Hill** are other manufacturers of note

Building Toys—**Lego**, **Tinker Toys**, **Erector Sets**
Celluloid, Cast Iron, Tin
Classic Toys—marbles, **Slinky**
TV, Movie, and Celebrity Toys
Wind-Up Toys
ViewMaster
Games

Not every toy from bygone eras goes up significantly in price. My friend Jim asked me to check on an item he had carefully stashed away in a closet, a 1980 **Rubik's Cube**, the famous puzzle invented by a Hungarian architecture professor in the 1970s, Mint in Box. We were both surprised and a little disappointed to find similar cubes only selling for eight to twelve dollars! It might have something to do with the fact that the Cube was such a phenomenal success; somewhere around 300 *million* Rubik's cubes were sold all over the world. Remember that scarcity factor!

## FIND OUT ABOUT TOYS

Toy price guides, information portals, and collector clubs are plentiful both on- and offline. *Toyzine* has articles, a directory of auctions and dealers, news, and listings of items for sale by collectors. The *Toy Cars Collectors Association* lists 962 manufacturers of diecast and other metal model cars on their website guides. Check out *The Diecast Car Collectors Zone* for auctions, events, and price archives.

Doll price guides are available for a variety of manufacturers. Denise Van Patten, the *About.com* doll guide, has written one called *The Official Price Guide to Dolls*, with 612 pages, and 900 photos! *Theriault's*, the premier auction company for dolls, offers doll education, catalogs, and gifts as well as online auctions.

**Webring** has a Toy Collectors site, which is accessible under Hobbies and Crafts—Collecting—Toys—and don't forget to search Google for toy clubs under "Groups." EBay has a buying guide for diecast vehicles with history and timelines.

## SELLING TOYS

If you have a valuable vintage toy or collection, arrange to have an evaluation by a specialized auction company such as *Bertoia* in Vineland, New Jersey. *Christie's* holds two sales a year just for teddy bears, and also has interests in dolls, Disneyana, dollhouses, and miniatures, trains, Barbie, and toy soldiers.

Toys are a good item to sell on eBay, since they are often lightweight and not difficult to pack. A typical day will show over 700,000 listings in Toys and Hobbies, with over 100,000 listings in Action Figures, the most popular category.

Vintage toys that turn out to be less valuable are perfect items for yard and garage sales, and may also be salable at antique malls. Donations of toys are always welcome at hospitals, shelters, clinics, and many other charities. Many local organizations such as *Moms* clubs have annual toy drives. Check out *Recycle.Net* for more ideas on donations and recycling used items.

# 11

# VINTAGE FASHION

K ate was in college when her grandmother, Grace, died. She helped
her parents clean out the modest home Grace had lived in for nearly
sixty years. Most of the furnishings and belongings were donated to local
charities, since Kate's mother, Nancy, thought that was what Grace would
have wanted. The house was put up for sale. Kate helped her mother pack
cartons one afternoon. One of her tasks was to empty the contents of a
heavy cedar chest.

"Do you know what's in it?" she asked, lifting the lid. The chest had
been in her grandmother's bedroom for as long as Kate could remember,
but she had never looked inside.

"I think it's probably drapes and bed linens," said Nancy. "Maybe some
old tablecloths and other things she never used, but stored away for some
reason."

The inside of the chest was fragrant with cedar and the scent of old,
perfumed sachets. Kate found some sheets piled neatly and began to take
them out. Beneath them, she saw edges of lace and embroidery. She pulled a
lightweight item from the neatly folded piles and drew her breath in sharply.
It was an antique piece of lingerie, a slip or nightshift. Kate marveled at the
delicacy of the satin and lace trim. Slowly she began to remove some of the
other delicate pieces of clothing, handling them carefully.

"Mom—you've got to see this!"

Nancy came into the room and looked at a lovely lace bed jacket Kate was holding up. "My goodness, Kate, those must be my grandmother's things. I remember now that Mother saved a few boxes of her clothes. They were very lovely quality and she hated to throw anything away. . . ."

"Your grandmother . . . Grandma's mother?"

"Yes, she was quite a lovely woman, from her pictures. Grandma's father had money before the stock market crash. These must have been expensive, and Grandma hated to discard them. Although no one wears anything like this anymore."

The chest contained a treasure-trove, Kate thought. Exquisite pieces of silk and delicate linen and damask; undergarments with intricate embroidery and lace details; drawers, negligees, petticoats, camisoles, corsets—some articles she didn't recognize.

Folded beneath the layers of undergarments were several dresses with beads and chiffon. As Kate held them up, she could tell they were in the low-waisted style of the 1920s. Some of the pieces had been mended with very great care, but most were in almost new condition.

"Mom, these things are so beautiful . . . we can't just give them away."

"What else is there to do with them?" Nancy wondered.

"Can I keep them? I'd love to have something that belonged to your grandmother."

"Of course you may have them. I don't know what you're going to do with them though."

Kate packed boxes of dresses and lingerie and put them in the closet of her room at home. She was busy at school, but when she came home to her parent's house on vacations, she often took the beautiful pieces out of the cartons and marveled at the details of the stitching and the beauty of the silk. She hung the beaded dresses, which were made for a taller woman, on the doors of her room to look at them, picturing glamorous balls and parties. As she grew older she thought of the collection less and less, although the packed boxes remained piled in her closet.

One day, years later, on a business trip to New York, Kate wandered into a vintage clothing boutique to look around. She nearly exclaimed out loud when she saw a few pieces of lingerie in a display case which reminded her of her grandmother's mementos.

"Can I help you?" Annie, the shop owner, looked up from behind the counter.

"Oh, I have some clothes similar to these. They belonged to my great grandmother."

"That piece—the ivory silk and lace—is from around 1920. Here, I'll take it out." Annie opened the case and Kate gasped when she turned over the price tag—the beautiful negligee was priced at over $700.

"I had no idea things like this were so expensive!"

"I'd love to see your collection. Why don't you take some photos and email them to me?"

Kate eventually consigned a number of pieces to Annie for sale in her shop. She was thrilled when Annie sent her a check for more than three thousand dollars. Annie also brokered a few other of Kate's pieces to a movie industry costumier. Kate's interest in vintage fashion began to grow. She scoured estate sales and flea markets looking for overlooked items of quality.

"It isn't so much the money," Kate said, "although that was exciting. I was pleased to sell these things to people who would value them. I had no idea of the marketplace—but now I do—and I'm always on the lookout for other vintage finds."

## VINTAGE FASHION HISTORY

The late country singer Patsy Cline would probably be glad, and not surprised, to know that her hit songs like "Crazy" were still being played and enjoyed today. What she might not have guessed, however, is that a red cowgirl style dress and jacket she often wore onstage auctioned at Christie's in November 2003 for $23,900.

Interest in vintage fashion has skyrocketed since 1949, when the Metropolitan Museum of Art in New York acquired the **Museum of Costume Art**, and established a department called the **Costume Institute**. The influential editor of *Vogue Magazine*, **Diana Vreeland**, was a special consultant to the Institute from 1972 until her death in 1989, and helped showcase the importance of textile and fashion design as a major decorative art form.

Royalty, stars, and celebrities have always been associated with high fashion.

**Princess Diana**'s celebrated June 1997, charity dress auction at Christie's raised over $3.25 million for cancer and AIDs charities, and showcased the intense interest among collectors for important fashion. **Marilyn Monroe**'s famous "Happy Birthday, Mr. President" flesh-colored sequined dress sold for a jaw-dropping $1.25 million in 1999. Vintage fashion collectors today include many movie and music stars, and more auction houses and museums now feature designer selections, not just from celebrity donors. From the work of important **couturiers** to vintage jeans and tennis shoes, fashion has become a hot ticket for collectors today.

## FASHION'S FOUNDING FATHERS

**Charles Worth**, an English draper who relocated to Paris in 1846, is considered the father of modern couture. Worth started designing dresses and bonnets for his wife, and other customers of the drapery shop started asking Worth for copies. With the help of a wealthy Swedish backer, Worth opened his first Paris dress making establishment. Soon his influential clients included the Empress Eugenie, wife of Emperor Napoleon III, the Austrian Princess de Metternich, and nobility from all over Europe as well as wealthy Americans. Worth was noted for his luxurious, opulent materials, flowing lines, and reinforced crinoline petticoats. The first fashion shows with live models were pioneered by Worth, and his fashion company was carried on by his heirs until the 1970s.

Worth, who died in 1895, inspired several future generations of designers. Worth's successors **Paul Poirot and Jean Patou**, **Mariano Fortuny**, **Coco Chanel**, **Jeanne Lanvin**, **Elsa Schiaparelli**, the **Callout sisters**, and **Christobel Balenciaga** were all important Parisian designers who shaped the early world of couture. In the post–World War II era, **Christian Dior** rose to importance with his modern creations that subtly invoked the luxurious and shapely form-fitting styles of the Victorian era.

In America, there had been little "high fashion" until the 1920s brought beginnings of an American style with the emergence of women's fashion magazines and the "flapper" or Jazz Age designs with short skirts and long waistlines.

With the coming of World War II, American designers were cut off from Paris and began to develop a style of their own, at first concentrating on sportswear and suits, combining femininity with practicality. One early important American dress designer of the 1940s was **Gilbert Adrian**, who had started in Paris but was brought to New York by the composer Irving Berlin to design costumes for Broadway shows. Adrian created Joan Crawford's famous broad-shouldered movie look of the 1940s and dressed other stars of the day such as Greta Garbo, Jean Harlow, and Katharine Hepburn.

By the 1950s and 1960s, both French and American designers were making fashion news. **Pierre Balmain, Pierre Cardin, Yves St. Laurent, Jacques Fath, Alix Gres, Norman Norell, Bill Blass**, and **Geoffrey Beene** were just a few of the important designers of the period.

New fabrics, pop culture, and a blend of elegance and casual lifestyle influenced fashion in the 1960s and 1970s. **Oleg Cassini**, an Italian-born Hollywood costume designer, gained importance as Jackie Kennedy's official couturier; French designer **Givenchy** was the first to market a luxury line of "ready to wear" fashions, which introduced a new generation of women to more affordable fashion they could buy in department stores. Other important names of the 1960s–1970s period were **Mary Quant, Emilio Pucci, Andre Courreges, Paco Rabanne, Halston, Zandra Rhodes**, and **James Galanos**.

## AT AUCTION

A 1950s gown by **Charles James** sold for $49,450, more than four times its original estimate, at Doyle's in April 1996. In May 2001, also at Doyle's, a stunning court-presentation dress designed by French fashion pioneer **Charles Frederick Worth** sold for over $101,000.

## WHAT'S IN *YOUR* CLOSET?

To be salable, vintage fashion items don't have to be haute couture or off a celebrity's back. *Au contraire*, many of us have valuable old clothes packed away (hopefully in mothballs) and don't even realize it.

## Dresses

Well-made **dresses and gowns** that are stylistically typical of their periods and in pristine condition can bring prices into the many hundreds. A designer label can increase value, but many haute couture creations are never labeled, and for many decades it was common to cut off labels. A vintage fashion expert can tell a *hand-stitched garment*, or sometimes identify fabrics and styles associated with certain designers. As with other antiques we have looked at, the oldest piece is not necessarily the most valuable.

Recently on eBay a 1920s brown chiffon flapper dress brought $219, an antique Victorian white lace wedding dress $179, and a very "type-y" 1950s scenic patterned white halter dress sold for over $500!

Claire, who runs a vintage fashion boutique, explained to me that prices can fluctuate depending on the current demand for particular styles, and the degree to which the dress exemplifies a period. She showed me a shapely 1950s black jumpsuit with cropped pants, rhinestone-accented appliques in poodle shapes, thin shoulder straps, and a boned bodice for support.

"Now, this outfit is *so fifties*, it has the poodles, which were 'the' dog of the period, it has the sexy upper top and cropped tapered pants. You can just see the girl wearing it, with a pony tail and red lipstick. It is also well made and it has a label. Although it is not an important designer, the piece is so typical, it will sell for a good price." I turned over the white cardboard price tag and saw that the outfit was priced to sell at $350!

"Fifties items sell well and they can be found in good condition," Claire went on to explain. "Right now some fifties items are going higher than well-made dresses from the twenties, but it would be a generalization to say that just because it is fifties, it will sell better than anything else. A lot of nice dresses from the 1970s are beginning to go up in value, and not just the top designers!"

## Vintage Fashion Values

I checked some more listings on eBay, as well as items for sale at online retailers after my visit with Claire. I found that many of the higher-priced completed items were in fact from the fifties. Many interesting dresses and other items were from earlier periods, such as an ivory two-piece c.

1910 Edwardian silk women's "walking suit," which sold for $271. Several vintage dresses from the forties with starting bids of $99.00 were going unsold, but the **Alfred Shaheen** form-fitting, late fifties/early sixties bright colored dresses with sexy halter tops were getting quick bids at that starting price.

Designs by **Emilio Pucci**, the Italian kingpin of beautiful vivid prints in luxurious silk and new stretchy synthetics made in the fifties and sixties were also getting snapped up, including an original bodysuit that was part of Pucci's Braniff Airline stewardess collection that went for $167.50.

## Lingerie

Undergarments like Kate's from all periods are fetching commanding prices online, at shows, and in shops.

I followed an eBay auction for a blue silk satin bustier corset similar to one of the items in Kate's collection—it sold for over $2500! Prices in the mid-hundreds are most common. Corsets and bustiers are the most popular sellers with petticoats, shifts, bed jackets, and other similar items attracting bids also.

## Hats

**Bes-Ben** (named for Bessie and Benjamin Greenfield) was the premier "celebrity" milliner of the 1940s and 1950s—the clientele included Lucille Ball, Judy Garland, Marlene Dietrich, and Elizabeth Taylor. Bes-Ben was known for chic, capped styles with veils, feathers, beads, fruits, flowers, and other trinkets. Bes-Ben hats can sell for anywhere from the low hundreds to several thousand; a couple of particularly fanciful models have sold famously in five figures.

## Handbags

The hottest designer bag on the market today, the Hermes Birkin Bag, is contemporary, overshadowing demand for some of its vintage cousins. But sixties and seventies **Louis Vuitton, Dior,** and **Gucci** bags in excellent condition can sell for several hundred dollars. **Alligator and other skin**

**bags** from the thirties through the fifties are particularly desirable, some bringing in the high hundreds to low thousands. Fifties **lucite**, **celluloid**, and "**box**" **purses** are popular; beaded bags from the 1920s and Victorian eras also sell well on eBay. An Art Nouveau purse with beautiful tortoise-shell colored plastic designs in beautiful condition with silk tassels and handles sold recently for over $1900. An antique embroidered purse with a Tiffany stamped silver clasp brought $455. A number of online vintage retailers had alligator and other skin bags in the $7–800 range.

## Shoes

Vintage **cowboy boots** are among the top sellers in the shoe category. Shoes must be in excellent, preferably near-mint condition to command highest prices, and quite a number of pairs top the $400 and $500 marks on eBay. Forties platform shoes in bright colors also are in demand, with several pairs priced over $150. Both men's and women's running shoes from the 1980s were getting plenty of action, especially the "**Air Jordan**" models. One pair of men's "first edition" Air Jordans sold for $1925. At a shop down the street from Claire's I saw a pair of antique Victorian lace-up shoes in excellent condition for $185, next to a pair of 1970s rainbow lucite "disco" high heels, asking price $125. Several of the vintage fashion websites I visited had pairs of 1950s "**saddle shoes**" in blue or brown and white, for around $75, and pairs of 1960s sueded pumps were going for around $36.

## Jeans

In 1873, **Levi Strauss**, a San Francisco dry goods merchant, and his tailor, Jacob Davis, received a patent for denim work pants with a riveted pocket, and the world has not been exactly the same since. At first the pants were made in blue denim and brown cotton "duck," but the brown cloth never softened and became comfortable, so it was discontinued. Strauss bought much of his blue cloth from Genoa, Italy, and started calling his pants "jeans" after "*genes*," the Italian word for the denim. Around 1890, the jeans were assigned the "batch" number **501**, which is still part of their name today. A competitor to Levis was begun in 1913 by Kansas entrepreneur **H. D. Lee**.

The 501 jeans are still manufactured by Levi Strauss, but early pairs, especially those made in the 1930s (Levi introduced its small red patch on the back pocket in 1936) through the 1950s, which can sell for anywhere from the hundreds to a few thousand dollars, particularly if they are unlaundered (hard to find in the average closet or dresser) or otherwise well-preserved. In 1971, Levi replaced the capital letter "E" in the LEVI logo with a small "e," and today the pairs with all-capitals are sought-after. That having been said, however—I saw a pair of mint-condition, unwashed, **1980s Levis Model 501As**, with original tags, even with the small letter "e," sell recently on eBay for $655.

## Men's Fashion

Besides Levis, popular collectible men's items include **Hawaiian shirts**, especially rayon, from the 1940s through the 1970s; **rock and roll jackets**, especially tour jackets and decorated leather jackets; 1920s–1930s "**gangster**" style jackets; and formal wear. Many vintage websites had Hawaiian shirts priced everywhere from $50 to $800; on eBay I saw several going in the $350 range with a few reaching the $600 area.

A vintage **Brooks Brothers** silk top hat, still in original box, sold on eBay for $195. A 1930s Lee sports jacket with a logo from a Princeton and Yale game brought over $700.

## Accessories

Desirable fashion accessories include **shawls**, **compacts**, **glasses** and **their cases**, **canes**, **lorgnettes (eyeglass holder)**, **belts**, **hosiery**, **gloves**, **fans**, and **scarves**. Alligator and crocodile purses (Claire showed me how to tell the difference: crocodile has little points or dots, which are actually hair follicles) can sell for anywhere from $100 to $1000, depending on condition and especially style. I saw several good examples on a specialty website, one **Gucci** green crocodile bag with brass clasp, lined with bright green kid skin, was $800 while a 1940s square purse with amber Bakelite trim was $900.

A pair of "Johnny Depp" type 1950s vintage horn-rim glasses sold for $1825 on eBay. Several pairs of vintage designer sunglasses—**Chanel** and **Balenciaga**—were going for between $200 and $300. (*Yes, really!*)

**Walking sticks** also seem popular—I saw several completed listings in different materials—ivory, rosewood, trimmed in brass and sterling, for over $400. A hand-painted silk and bone-handle ladies fan sold for $355.


## FASHION LINGO

Many fashion terms refer to types of fabrics or elements of design:

Barathea—soft fabric of wool, silk/cotton, or silk/wool blend with various weaves

Battenburg—a Renaissance-style lace

Bodice—originally a brassiere or undergarment, the word now refers to the upper section of a dress or jacket

Bustier—camisole

Chambray—yarn-dyed plain-weave fabric with white filling

Clutch—a small hand-held purse

Crepe—any fabric with a crimped or grained surface

Crepe de chine—lightweight, usually silk crepe

Decollete—low-cut neckline

Dolman sleeve—a sleeve wide at the armhole narrowing to the wrist, sometimes a variation is called a batwing sleeve

Empire—waistline starting just beneath the bust

Epaulet—an extra strap of material sewn across a shoulder

Faille—a dressy, flat-ribbed fabric with a light luster

Georgette—sheer lightweight plain-weave fabric

Jacquard—woven or knitted fabric made on the first type of automated loom invented in 1801 by Joseph Marie Jacquard allowing for more complexity in woven patterns

Maillot—women's one-piece bathing suit

Mantle or mantelet—a cloak or cape of various lengths

Merino—high-quality wool yarn made from the fleece of Merino sheep

Pagoda sleeve—a sleeve narrow at the top and widely flared from elbow to wrist

Raglan sleeve—a sleeve extending to the neckline

Set-in sleeve—a sleeve sewn into the natural armhole

Shagreen—a leather made from sharkskin or other exotic fish (such as stingray) skin—*not to be confused with*:

Shaheen (Alfred)—a 1960s designer famous for Asian-inspired prints and bright colors

Shantung—medium-weight silk-like fabric made with uneven or nubby yarns

Shirring—a gathering to create soft folds in a garment

Toile—light/medium cotton type fabric with print design—*not to be confused with*:

Voile—a lightweight, often sheer fabric

## FIND OUT ABOUT FASHION

If you want to learn more about the details of collecting vintage fashion, you can get more information than you can imagine from the eBay Fashion Collectors Club or the Vintage Clothing and Accessories Discussion Board.

*The Costume Society of America* is an online symposium with a list of fashion research libraries, scouts, researchers, books, and periodicals. *The Vintage Fashion Guild* has label research, fashion and designer history, and public forums. *Virtual Vintage* by Linda Lindroth and Deborah Newell Tornello has listings of over one hundred top vintage sites and ideas about how to sell online.

Look for a vintage fashion expert at a fashion and costume show or try a local museum. Many art museums such as the **Los Angeles County Museum of Art** and the **Cincinnati Art Museum** now have permanent costume and textile arts departments. **The Costumer's Manifesto** has links to museums and collections all over the world, designer resources, and vintage clothing retailers.

## WHAT TO DO WITH VINTAGE FASHION

Vintage fashion and resale shops have sprouted everywhere, and this is one area where consignments are often welcome. Many of the dealers I spoke with consign or purchase at the rate of 40% of retail selling price. Some shops will donate your clothes to charity for you and obtain receipts if your items don't sell in a period agreed to.

EBay has a busy marketplace for vintage fashion. On several days when I checked, there were over 160,000 active listings. Make sure you list in the right category or use keywords in your listing that refer to period, designer or manufacturer, and materials.

*Selling Tip*: Vintage fashion experts recommend that you invest in a display mannequin or dress form to photograph your clothes. You can get one from a **store fixtures wholesaler** or possibly find a used one on eBay. Take *detailed* measurements and note the condition of typical-wear areas such as hems, underarms, and necklines.

Clothes and shoes are always welcome as donations if they prove not to be salable. Most charities accept them, some special needs might exist at homeless shelters and relief organizations. I heard of one organization that was helping inner-city women "dress for success" while making transitions into the workforce. Theatrical departments of schools and colleges might also welcome costume and wardrobe donations.

# 12

# MEMORABILIA

As a college student in the late 1960s, Mickey was obsessed with rock and roll. Late each night his dorm room would pulsate with Cream, Bob Dylan, The Rolling Stones, Jefferson Airplane, the Grateful Dead. He and his friends hitchhiked around the East Coast attending concerts.

Mickey began saving his concert ticket stubs, T-shirts, and other souvenirs of the events. He papered the walls of his room with flyers and posters. He stuffed his belongings into a duffel bag and bought a cardboard tube for the posters when he ran out of wall space.

One evening Mickey struck up a conversation with one of the equipment crew loading amplifiers onto a trailer truck. Before long, he had been hired for the summer as part of the road crew for one of his favorite bands. Life on the road with a rock band was fun. When he graduated, Mickey decided to put off going to law school and work in the music business for a while. He toured with several bands as a road manager, then an assistant for a concert producer, and even worked for a recording company helping out in the studio.

Mickey's parents watched his rock career blossoming with chagrin. They nagged him frequently about his plans to become a lawyer. Eventually

Mickey entered law school and became an attorney, planning to focus on the music industry. Although he still enjoyed attending concerts and listening to music, Mickey gradually became interested in corporate and financial law, in takeovers and public offerings. He married and became a father, and joined a prestigious law firm. Over time, his days on the road and in the studio became a distant memory.

Mickey still kept several tubes of concert posters and knapsacks and duffel bags of items he had saved from his rock and roll days. His souvenirs included autographs, photos, recordings, original drawings, letters, songs and poems written on planes and buses, signed for Mickey by his rock heroes. He also had jackets and T-shirts from tours, and other curios such as belt buckles and jewelry engraved for musicians, who had gotten tired of the baubles and given them away.

His New York apartment was spacious, but the closets had little room for extra storage. One weekend he arrived at his parents' home with several cartons of law books, old clothes, and the music memorabilia, and asked his parents to store his belongings in the basement for him.

"Some day when I've got a big house in the Hamptons, I'll come back for this stuff," he promised them.

Years passed. Mickey had become a successful corporate attorney. His own children were grown and starting careers. Mickey's parents were aging, and they decided to sell their home and move to a retirement community in Florida.

One day Mickey received a call from his mother.

"Mom, can I call you on the weekend? I'm in the middle of merger talks."

"Mickey, I found some old bags and boxes of yours in the basement. The movers are coming on Monday. What do you want me to do with this old stuff?"

Mickey recalled vaguely the collection of rock souvenirs. He knew there were tapes in the duffel bags that might be valuable, but they would have to be remastered on today's equipment. He couldn't remember what else there was. Some old posters he used to pull down off the telephone poles and from the theater lobbies. There certainly wasn't time to drop an important negotiation and rush out to the suburbs to load his car with bags and boxes he had no room to store.

"Mom, let me get back to you. I'll let you know."

"Mickey, the movers are coming on Monday. Anything we don't take is going to be sold at a garage sale. The two nice young men down the street are going to have one for us."

Mickey was distracted by his secretary, who signaled he had two incoming calls. "Mom, it's okay. Do what you think is best. I'll fly down to Florida the week after next and help you get settled."

The young neighbors who lived down the street from Mickey's parents, Jim and Jake, came over the following day to help sort through property for the garage sale.

"Oh, and those bags and boxes down in the basement, there are some things that belonged to my son."

Jim and Jake went down to the basement and looked through the cartons of Mickey's law books. They unzipped the first of the duffel bags. The first item they lifted out was a Led Zeppelin T-shirt signed: "To Mickey—Jimmy Page." Programs, concert ticket stubs, backstage passes, autographed albums, signed photos, and magazines were packed underneath. Jim unfurled the posters from one of the cardboard tubes, marvelling that most of them were in excellent condition.

"This stuff is worth thousands," breathed Jim.

They stared at each other for a moment in silence.

"We can't just sell this at a garage sale," Jake said. "Look, there are tapes in here. Professional quality. Done in a studio."

"We should tell the guy. He must remember this stuff. We can sell it for him on eBay and give him a percentage."

Mickey was surprised and relieved to hear from Jim and Jake that his collection had not perished at a yard sale. They offered to catalog his belongings and contact some record producers specializing in archives about the tapes. When they began listing items on eBay, they received a flood of emails and inquiries from collectors around the world. Even Jim and Jake had not known the demand for historical rock items.

As a surprise gift to Mickey, they decided to have a few special items mounted and framed. When the eBay auctions were completed, Jim and Jake went to Mickey's office with the framed gift, an accounting of the items sold, and his check for the share of the eBay proceeds. Jim and Jake had received almost $50,000 in gross proceeds.

Mickey hung the framed collection on the wall of his office and drew up a contract for Jim and Jake to participate in proceeds from the archived recordings. He donated his share of the eBay money to a favorite charity.

"The money's not the important thing," Mickey told them. "This was a part of my life that had faded into the past. It might have been lost forever if not for you two. Now some of my things belong to people who will value them—maybe some of it will even wind up in a museum some day!"

## MEMORABILIA IS HOT

The dictionary defines "memorabilia" as "individual items of historical value." Some pieces of memorabilia are souvenirs or commemorative gifts made in honor of a person, place, or event, such as a royal wedding or world's fair. But other pieces fall into the category of commonplace objects: a set of odd buttons from Civil War uniforms, for instance, were appraised recently at $2500 on the *Antiques Roadshow*. A porcelain sign from an old MobilOil gas station was valued at $4000.

## MOVIE, MUSIC, AND ENTERTAINMENT MEMORABILIA

Recently a lock of hair purportedly from Marilyn Monroe's head, complete with a notarized "affadavit of authenticity" (supposedly from her embalmer!) was auctioned on eBay for over $500. The more mainstream, but never dull, types of entertainment memorabilia include:

### Autographs

On photos, documents, letters, and cards, even on napkins, virtually on anything, **autographs** have always been a favorite of collectors. This category might include a contract signed by a star for a famous film or other legal documents. Some collectors will buy almost anything with a famous signature—one internet Elvis memorabilia site was offering a signed property conveyance document for Elvis's purchase of Graceland in 1957—asking price, $60,000!

## Posters

Some of the highest prices for entertainment items have been in the poster category. The market seems to value most highly the horror movie heroes—**Boris Karloff, Bela Lugosi**, of the 1930s—the all-time record sale for a movie poster was in 1997, when a poster for Boris Karloff in *The Mummy* sold at Sotheby's for $453,000. Others on the top-ten list include *King Kong, Casablanca, Dracula, Bride of Frankenstein*, and *Gone with the Wind*.

An average price for a popular vintage poster in good condition can vary. A 1961 poster from the film *Breakfast at Tiffany's* was appraised on the *Antiques Roadshow* for $5000, and one sold on eBay for a Buy-It-Now price of $3000 in a matter of hours. Another poster, featuring **James Cagney** in *The G-Men*, was appraised on *Roadshow* for $25,000 because of its rarity. **James Bond, Star Wars, Elvis**, and **horror** still seem to be some of the most sought-after posters.

**Lobby art, ads, playbills, and promotional stills** from famous movies are also attracting buyers.

## Costumes, Scripts, and Props

Things that were actually used and handled by the stars of a famous film during its making are hot items. A shooting script from the John Wayne movie, *The Quiet Man*, sold for $960 on eBay in 2005. A final shooting script from the 1954 Alfred Hitchcock thriller, *To Catch a Thief*, with Cary Grant, sold the same week for $782.

An unsigned copy of a script from a Humphrey Bogart movie, *The Harder They Fall*, was bid at $100; a script with the late Michael Landon's signature from his TV series show, *Little House on the Prairie*, was selling for $75.

---

## AT AUCTION

**M**arlon Brando's personal copy of his script for *The Godfather* broke a record when it sold for $312,800 at Sotheby's in June 2004, toppling the $244,500 sale of **Clark Gable**'s *Gone with the Wind* script in 1996. Possibly the most famous movie costume ever sold at auction, **Judy Garland**'s gingham dress from *The Wizard of Oz*, brought the hammer down for $252,000 at Bonham's in April 2005.

---

## CELEBRITY BELONGINGS, NOVELTIES, TV SHOW EPHEMERA

This category can include furnishings from famous homes, personal affects, clothing, and belongings. Roslyn Herman, a New York dealer in celebrity articles, offered such items on her website as a pair of Marlon Brando's cufflinks ($225)—a white mesh purse owned by **Barbara Stanwyck** ($195), and a selection of pieces of **Jean Harlow**'s art deco jewelry ranging from $200 to $400. A trademark hat belonging to comic **Red Skelton** auctioned on eBay for $275. A denim jacket **Elvis** wore in the 1957 movie *Loving You*, complete with Paramount Studios wardrobe stamp, auctioned in October 2004 for $10,627.

### Cast and Crew Jackets

Never worn onscreen, but by the production team! For popular movies, especially the **Star Wars** series, cast and crew jackets can sell for anywhere from $50 to $300.

### Novelty Merchandise

Memorabilia associated with famous movies and TV shows—coasters, glasses, cigarette lighters, keychains, costumes—is also collectible. Shows like **Star Trek** have their own "galaxy" of memorabilia items as well!

## Rock and Pop Items

In 2004, three-time Rock and Roll Hall of Fame inductee **Eric Clapton**, the renowned lead guitarist, auctioned a collection of his guitars at Christie's to benefit a rehab center he had established. The most important guitar in the collection, Clapton's famous 1957 Fender Stratocaster, nicknamed "Blackie," sold for an incredible $959,500. The late Grateful Dead bandleader **Jerry Garcia**'s guitars also brought prices in the $700–900,000 range at Guernsey's, in New York in 2002.

---

### AT AUCTION

Lyrics from the **Beatles**' song "Revolution" with John Lennon's notes sold for 72,000 British pounds or around $133,000 at Bonham's April 2005 Rock, Pop, and Film Memorabilia Sale.

---

Other valuable rock items, similar to the items in Mickey's collection, include:

Signed photos—the Beatles and Elvis usually top the "charts" in this category

Clothes—jackets associated with KISS, Guns & Roses, Led Zeppelin, and Bruce Springsteen all are popular sellers, whether or not it can be proven that the jacket ever graced the back of the rocker in question himself—also jewelry, belts, and T-shirts, especially tour and backstage.

Tickets, backstage passes, programs, tour posters—An unused ticket to the Beatles' August 15, 1965, concert at Shea Stadium in near-mint condition sold on eBay for $3100 in June 2005.

## DISNEYANA

Disney collectibles have their own category. Many books, stores, catalogs, and even museum exhibitions have been devoted to Disney memorabilia.

Valuable Disney items include **toys and dolls**—a vintage Steiff Mickey Mouse doll with tags, buttons, and blue pants (supposedly the rarest in Mickey's wardrobe) sold for $13,700 at a Barrett's auction in 2003; another in brown pants was featured in Judith Miller's *2004 Collectibles Price Guide* at $5–7000.

Other sought-after Disney items include **lead and diecast toys, mechanical banks, bisque figurines** (early ones were distributed by the George Borgfeldt doll company), **tins, lunch boxes, books** (Mickey Mouse Studios, Whitman and Random House were early publishers), **magazines, glasses, party games**, and **tin lithographed beach pails**; advertising cartons and other promotional **packaging** for food products; back-to-school items like **pencil boxes, paint sets, and crayons; drinking mugs** and **cereal bowls**; and the **famous Ingersoll watches** and **clocks**.

Much Disney memorabilia was reproduced starting in the 1980s and is still made today for sale in gift shops, and at the Disney resorts and cruise ships and other venues.

## ANIMATION ART

**Animation art** is in a collectible category all its own. It has relationships both to art and to movie memorabilia. Animation art includes **original art**, also called "**production art**" because it actually was used in making the original animated film, and **reproduction art**.

Original animation art has been collected since the 1930s, when a savvy San Francisco art dealer named Guthrie Courvoisier convinced Walt Disney that he could market original **animation cels** from Disney's 1937 blockbuster film, *Snow White and the Seven Dwarfs*, to his wealthy collectors. Exhibits at exclusive galleries in New York and London followed. By 1940 the cels, principally from *Snow White* but from a few other films as well, had been added to the permanent collections of over twenty museums, including New York's Metropolitan Museum and the Museum of Modern Art's film library.

After the late 1940s, the novelty wore off temporarily for collectors, and during the 1950s and 1960s, the artwork was sold at Disneyland, often for less than $5 apiece!

By the late 1970s and 1980s, interest from fine galleries had picked up again. The **Whitney Museum of American Art** in New York held its first important Disney animation art exhibit in 1981, and the first Christie's auction exclusively devoted to animation art followed in 1984. Disney was not the only collectible animator; others include **Hanna Barbera**, famous for the Flintstones, **Fleischer Studios**, who produced Popeye, and **Warner Brothers**.

There are three different types of original animation art:

- original, hand-painted production cels, on acetate—cels from the 1930s, before more durable acetate was used, are scarce;
- drawings, which may be black pencil sketches or fully colored, illustrated scenes and backgrounds; and
- pre-production art, which includes storyboards, paintings and drawings, and concept scenes.

Cels themselves are not usually signed unless mounted for presentation, but a large number of drawings, paintings, and storyboards were signed by the artists or production personnel.

Cels can be worth anywhere from a few hundred dollars to over $100,000, depending on their size, complexity, date, whether they contain a completed background, and other factors. Rare Mickey Mouse and Donald Duck cels have sold for between $200,000 and $500,000. Average prices for cels from important Disney films like *Snow White* can be in the $4–10,000 range.

Animation art **reproductions** began in the 1970s and 1980s. They include handpainted **limited editions**, **seri-cels**, or **silkscreens**, often called "**limited edition cels**," and "**giclees**" or reproductions of paintings on paper or board. They're considered modern collectibles, and shouldn't be confused with original art.

## HISTORICAL MEMORABILIA

Historical memorabilia includes letters, documents, photos, antique personal objects, and other unusual things! A letter or document with a signature of a famous figure like Abraham Lincoln might bring over $100,000 at any auction; but collectors are also interested in a wide range of items of historical significance.

---

### AT AUCTION

Honest Abe is the record holder for historical documents; in March 2002, an autographed copy of **Lincoln**'s last public speech brought $3,086,000 at Christie's.

At the same sale (from Malcolm Forbes's collection) another bidder paid $160,000 for **Paul Revere**'s expense ledger, including billing for his famous "ride."

A previously unpublished **Beethoven** manuscript on a single page sold for $273,440 at Sotheby's in 1999.

---

If you browse the historical memorabilia category on eBay, you will see all kinds of interesting items. An 1893 Chicago World's Fair coin bank, an 1860 copy of *Harper's* magazine covering the presidential election, a 1937 military photo album, tin portraits of Russian Czar Nicholas and his wife Alexandra, some antique fire station equipment, and a vintage American Legion lapel pin were all items with multiple bids on a recent quick search I did.

## MILITARY

Military items of all kinds are collectible; perhaps the most important area of "militariana" is the **Civil War**, but items from **World Wars I and II**, **Nazi** items, military items from all sorts of cultures and civilizations are popular.

**Civil War memorabilia** can include everything from ammunition (such as bullets and cartridge boxes) to accoutrements (items the soldiers carried—canteens, knapsacks, leather goods, camping and cooking items)—also belts, coins, currency, medical equipment, newspapers, flags, insignias, pieces of uniforms, buttons, photos, letters, documents, and maps.

**Battlefield relics**, items actually retrieved from battle sites, are highly collectible and may consist of only fragments of bullets, bayonet tips, parts and pieces of guns, and other equipment.

Guns, knives, swords, and other **weapons** are a specialized area; there are dealers who specialize in these as well as military documents, maps, manuals, and pamphlets. Field gear, uniforms, coins, and all types of equipment and instruments are also of interest.

I was amazed to see some of the prices for pieces of military gear going by on eBay on a typical day. A Confederate canteen in a leather sling was snapped up for $1625, a vintage horse gas mask with all the trappings sold with fifteen bids for $1525. A metal ship's plaque from a WWII naval tugboat was bought for $2175. Swords are particularly hot items; several ranging from a U.S. Navy Civil War sword to a Japanese officer's sabre sold in the $6000 range. A U.S. 7th Navy Beach Battalion helmet, which was said to have been worn on D-Day, attracted bids up to $4400.

**Medals** were particularly sought after; a WWII Purple Heart medal with its original case and documents, awarded to a U.S. paratrooper killed in Holland, sold for $2158.

Clothing and parts of uniforms, especially epaulets and patches, were attracting lots of action; several bomber jackets were selling for $3–500, a Civil War Maryland Militia belt buckle for $2000 (while a "Civil War era" buckle sold for over $200) and a pair of Napoleonic War leather pants were hotly bid up to $1100.

## POLITICAL CAMPAIGN

Historians say that Andrew Jackson was the first candidate running for office who got the idea to give out small medals or tokens that could be pinned to your lapel as a way of showing support for the candidate of your choice! The next innovation was called a **"ferrotype,"** a photographic image on a thin sheet or tin or iron inserted into a brass frame to be pinned on. The first **modern-style campaign buttons**, paper images wrapped onto a metal disk and coated with transparent celluloid, were seen in the McKinley-Bryan presidential campaign of 1896.

Other than buttons, **campaign memorabilia** can include a variety of small objects like pens and pencils, sewing notions, watch fobs, paperweights, posters and fliers, even toys. Several presidents, including **Bill Clinton**, have been avid collectors of political memorabilia, and a nonprofit group called **American Political Items Collectors** has over three thousand members.

Some collectors specialize in a particular figure, such as Teddy Roosevelt or JFK, others in a certain era, or something such as First Lady material. With the establishment of several presidential libraries in the past few decades, interest in historical political items has grown. Many universities, such as **Duke**, as well as the **Smithsonian**, also maintain collections.

Stan saved a collection of Kennedy and Nixon buttons from the sixties and seventies, and asked me to check the prices on these. I found that **Franklin Roosevelt** was topping the price list for campaign buttons on eBay, with a collection of ten going for over $2200. Kennedy buttons were surprisingly low, in the $20–30 range, with rare and less-heard-of candidates such as **Alton Parker** (who ran against Teddy Roosevelt in 1904—and no, I never heard of him either!) going for well over $300. Remember: rarity and scarcity!

**Martin Van Buren** material, for example, is considered hard to find, and a flag depicting **Rutherford B. Hayes** sold for $30,000 at an auction in 2000.

## ADVERTISING AND INDUSTRIAL MEMORABILIA

An empty jar of Planters Peanuts? A 1920s Sunshine Biscuit tin? A paper bookmark with the Pears Soap logo? Yes (you should know this by now) collectors buy all these items and more. Advertising memorabilia can be something as simple as an old food can.

**Tins** were used to package food and other items such as tobacco from the 1860s until the 1930s, when less expensive forms of packaging such as cardboard prevailed. The more brightly colored and artistic designs bring higher prices, not only of tins and other food containers, but paper advertisements (called "**broadsides**"), display signs, trade cards, punchcards, display figures, and advertising novelty items such as ash trays, utensils, and figurines.

Collectible brands include **Sunshine**, **Planters**, **Pears' Soap**, and **Guinness**, familiar names today, which are in demand, but collectors also gravitate to defunct companies—**Sexton's Cocoa, Banner Baking Powder**, and **Bickmore's Morticians' Powder** ("Allay All Disagreeable Odors") were some of the tins and containers featured in Judith Miller's *2004 Collectibles Price Guide*, all selling for between $100 and $300. Another guide I checked featured a **Samoset Chocolate** tin and an ad placard for "**Dr. Lash's Bitters**"—both priced in the $2–4000 range!

**Coca Cola** is famous for its tin advertising trays, which can sell for anywhere from $50 into the thousands, and Coke porcelain fountain signs can bring anywhere from $500 to $2000. Signs and placards, toys (including miniature trucks and cars), glassware, bottle caps, match boxes, and countless other advertising trinkets bring prices from a few dollars to a few thousand. The most valuable Coke memorabilia is from the 1880s through the 1890s, but material from the early 1900s up through the 1930s is also desirable.

Beer company memorabilia, called "**breweriana**" can also be of value. Some of the popular and familiar names here include **Hamm's**, **Bruck's**, **Schlitz**, **Coors**, and **Budweiser**, but as with other advertising items, some of the highest priced items include less familiar or now-defunct brands such as **Ashland.**

Firearms and fishing tackle companies produced some of the most beautifully executed advertising art. **Winchester, Colt, Marlin, Remington, Hercules Gun Powder**, and **DuPont** engaged popular artists of the early twentieth century such as **N. C. Wyeth, A. Russell, Frederic Remington, A. B. Frost**, and **Philip R. Goodman** to create beautiful illustrations for packaging, cardboards, advertising brochures, catalogs, posters, and promotional items such as calendars.

"**Petroliana**" refers to items which often are pieces and parts of old gas stations themselves—porcelain and metal signs, globes, gas pumps. On eBay, I saw a case of old Shell glass motor oil bottles (empty now) in their original metal carrier sell for close to $1000, with thirty bidders involved! Now, if I had found that item rummaging through an old garage before studying up on memorabilia, it would have very likely ended up in the trash!

## TRAVEL MEMORABILIA

People seem to have a fascination with old trains, steamships, and other modes of transport. Objects from some of the luxurious ocean liners from the early 1900s such as china, postcards, dining menus, ash trays, ship documents, and logs, have all been finding their way into collections as of late. Anything from the ill-fated *Titanic* or opulent *Mauritania* is the "gold standard" in this category. Similar items from vintage railway lines are called—you know this one by now—**railroadiana!**

## FAMOUS EVENTS AND COMMEMORATIVE

World's Fairs, royal weddings and coronations, inaugurations, many news-worthy events of the past were promoted with such items as plaques, plates, mugs, cups and saucers, gift tins, brochures, pins, buttons, maps and guides, tokens, medallions, paperweights, and just about any other kind of item you can think of!

A **Queen Elizabeth II coronation cup and saucer**, similar to one I received from my grandmother as a child, was featured on the Time Was Antiques website selling for $80. A **Prince Charles and Princess Diana wedding paper-doll book** ($118), a **Queen Victoria jubilee medal** ($80), and a **King George VI Royal Doulton** coronation urn ($360) are other examples.

## SPORTS MEMORABILIA

Sports collectibles is one of the most explosive markets of today, and baseball is the hot ticket.

---

### AT AUCTION

In December 2004, one of the highest priced pieces of sports mem-orabilia was auctioned at Sotheby's. A bat used by **Babe Ruth** at Yankee Stadium in 1923, later signed by the Babe and dedicated to a home-run-hitting student in Los Angeles, sold for a record $1.265 million. In May 2005, a jersey worn by famous New York Yankee Mickey Mantle in a 1954 game was sold for $119,500 at Heritage.

---

## BASEBALL CARDS

Baseball cards began shortly after Major League Baseball was established, in 1869. No one knows exactly who made the first card, but the first known cards inserted into cigarette and tobacco packages appeared in the 1880s. **Goodwin and Company** of New York was one of the first, if not the first, to get the idea. In the early 1900s, the **American Tobacco Company** began to issue the bright-colored cards of baseball heroes to try to get an edge on some newfound competition brought about by antitrust regulations.

Early tobacco cards from this period are identified with a letter "T" and a number. The "**T206**" set issued between 1909 and 1911 is legendary for its scarcity and color lithography. The **Honus Wagner card from the T-206** set is among the most rare and collectible baseball card of all time—some say because Wagner was opposed to tobacco and ordered his cards removed from the packages. One of these cards sold for $640,000 to an investor in 1996 at Christie's; the buyer auctioned the card on eBay in 2000 for a record $1.1 million—the first baseball card ever to reach such a price.

With the advent of **third-party grading,** many cards from the 1930s through the 1970s have risen in price to astounding four- and five-figure prices. **Goudey, George C. Miller, DeLong**, and **National Chicle** first made cards in a 2 1/4-inch format in the 1930s. In the forties, **Bowman and Leaf** was prevalent until a gigantic new competitor, **Topps Chewing Gum**, emerged and dominated the baseball card market until antitrust rulings allowed for more competition in 1980.

Other collectible baseball items include gloves, jackets, pieces of uniforms, yearbooks, programs, photographs, old tickets, souvenirs, and scorecards. Other sports such as golf, boxing, car racing, and football, just to name a few, also have their share of collectible items.

**Fishing** memorabilia is a special sports category. Yes, fishing! **Lures, reels**, and the boxes and cabinets that store them are key areas of fishing collectibles. If I found a box of fishing lures in a garage, the last thing I would think is that a wooden lure **(1903 Heddon high forehead underwater minnow)** auctioned in Texas in 1998 for $9500. Oh, and be careful of that box of wooden duck decoys over there in the corner—the *Maine Antique Digest* reports regularly on the **Guyette & Schmidt** Annual Spring Decoy Auction, where the top price for a waterfowl in 2002 was $34,650.

## FIND OUT ABOUT MEMORABILIA

**Museums, archives, foundations, and special collections** for historical materials exist all over the country—John Philip Sousa's manuscripts, for example, have been preserved at the University of Illinois. Coca Cola has a special museum in Kentucky. Hollywood stars such as Ava Gardner and Laurel and Hardy have their own museums, as do *Gone with the Wind* author Margaret Mitchell and many major sports teams.

Major auction houses now conduct memorabilia auctions frequently; Christie's has specialist areas in maritime objects, sports collectibles, and entertainment. *Heritage Galleries* and *Hake's* are two smaller and more specialized auction companies dealing in memorabilia. *Mastronet* conducts online auctions with bidding by telephone.

*PSA (Professional Sports Authenticator)* is the principal third-party grading firm for baseball cards and autographed sports collectibles. On their site *PSACARD* you can read auction news results, browse message boards, join a collector club, or find links to dealers. Online "museums" like *Railroadiana.Org* provide extensive coverage of category-specific memorabilia and history; the *Center for the Study of the Civil War* has links to extensive Civil War resources on the web.

Large collections of memorabilia are sometimes purchased by libraries, museums, and certain investors. Historical societies and local museums are a good place to contact for reference. Occasionally auction companies might act as brokers in private sales. For celebrity items, fan clubs are a good place to ask questions—run a Google search to see if there are websites devoted to the famous person. Many new museums and collections of rock, historical, and celebrity items are springing up every day.

## WHAT TO DO WITH MEMORABILIA

**Provenance** is extremely important with memorabilia, so always be careful to preserve evidence of authenticity of an item.

Remember to try not to clean or repair anything you find; if you have packs of baseball cards bound by rubber bands you can remove the bands, being careful not to cause tears. Save any scraps of paper or notes. Don't erase any writing on any item, as it may be a clue to the vintage and origin of the article. Any materials on paper, including letters and photographs, should not be handled too extensively. Make photocopies very carefully or take digital photos, and use the copies if you are going to show things to any experts in advance of having materials evaluated or appraised.

**Archival materials** are available to help safely store, mount, and display valuable items—**Archival Products**, **Gaylord**, and **Conservation Resources** are only a few of the companies you can contact for information.

## MEMORABILIA VALUES

Many pieces of memorabilia are unique, and present special challenges for valuation and appraisal. Comparable sales might be few or nonexistent, so auction companies and appraisers may be cautious when attempting to establish estimates. Condition is also of great importance, especially with historical and advertising items that have been used and handled.

Some famous auctions of celebrity items in recent years—such as the February 2005 Sotheby's sale of household items belonging to John F. Kennedy—have generated publicity for sky-high prices, such as the sale of JFK's rocking chair for $96,000 and a golf club for $65,750. Research into the later values of these items showed that once the "buying fever" of the celebrity auction passed, many of the pieces were resold for substantially lower prices. The popularity of media heroes in our modern age may rise and fall, and the prices of their belongings may bear similarity to the internet stock bubble of the late 1990s when viewed in hindsight!

The best thing you can do with a memorabilia collection or special piece is to get a variety of opinions and evaluations. Learning more about what is collectible will help you evaluate what kind of potential market exists for your category of treasures.

# 13

# STAMPS, COMICS, PHOTOS, AND OTHER PAPER PASTIMES

## STAMPS

Postage stamps, unlike coins and pottery, are a relatively modern invention! Down through history, postage for items sent through the mail was usually collected upon delivery.

In 1840, Sir Rowland Hill, British postmaster general under Queen Victoria, created the first adhesive postal stamp (bearing the likeness of Her Majesty) and established the price to mail a letter at one penny. This first-ever stamp, known as "The Penny Black," was unveiled on May 6, 1840, and was an instant success. Over 68 million Penny Blacks were issued, and it is estimated that over 1.5 million survive today. That should tell you something about its collectible value—a used Penny Black can be acquired for around $150.

The concept quickly caught on in all civilized countries of the world. The United States issued its first stamps in 1847, a **5-cent Ben Franklin** and a **10-cent George Washington**. At first stamp sheets were not perforated, and had to be cut at the post office. In 1855 perforation became standard.

Stamp collecting is one of the most popular hobbies in the world. At one time, the U.S. Postal Service estimated that there were close to 20 million stamp collectors in the United States alone, a number that is in some dispute. Stamps are a popular activity among young people, and there are thought to be thousands of organizations for collectors young and old, including school, church, neighborhood, and Cub Scout clubs.

## COLLECTIBLE STAMP ITEMS

**"Philately"** means the study of stamps. A "philatelist" is not necessary a collector, but someone who does research and accumulates knowledge about the finer points of stamps, of which there are many.

The value of a stamp depends partly on its age, but also on its rarity. Older stamps from before 1935 (some collectors say 1925) are generally the most sought-after. Stamps may occur in collections in mint (uncancelled) state or used (cancelled)—and may have different values in either state.

Collectible stamp items include the **postage stamps** themselves, both used and unissued; **"covers,"** meaning envelopes with stamps on them; **"first day covers,"** envelopes postmarked on the first day a stamp went into use; and **"cachets,"** decorated versions of first day covers that commemorate the stamp. The Post Office began announcing "first days of issue" for stamps in the 1920s, and early first day covers were simply ordinary envelopes used to mail letters with the stamps postmarked on the first official day of use.

Cachets, commercially produced and popularized by influential philatelist George W. Linn in 1923, can involve drawings, engravings, lithography, photography, laser printing, and so forth. Cachets are considered an art form, and there are several major cachet making companies today who design and produce them in editions ranging from the thousands to tens of thousands.

**Blocks and strips** of stamps are also collectible and can be more valuable, especially when older and more scarce.

## STAMP LINGO

Stamp collecting is full of exotic and complicated terms like **"roulette,"** **"omnibus,"** **"tete-beche,"** **"coil line pairs"** and other nearly incomprehensible things. Stamps are full of small secrets and minor variations that can be seen only through a magnifying glass. If you are going to have dealings with any stamp dealers, it's best to make a small investment in a guidebook, such as ***How to Collect Stamps*** from H. E. Harris and Company. A good guide to stamps will have a glossary for ready reference.

A few common terms you are apt to hear:

Block—an unseparated group of stamps at least two high and two wide

Cancellation—a postal authority mark showing the stamp was used for mailing

Coils—stamps issued in rolls one stamp wide

Denomination—the postage value of the stamp

Error—a stamp with something incorrect in the design or manufacture

Frank—marking on the face of a cover indicating it is to be delivered

Gum Condition—the state of the adhesive on the back of the stamp

Hinged—attached to a page in a stamp album

Laid Paper—paper with crossed lines that can be seen when held up to light

Pictorial—a stamp with a picture other than a portrait or static design

Reprint and Reissue—a stamp printed from its original plate after it is no longer valid for postage

Selvage—unprinted paper margin around the stamp

Strip—three or more unseparated stamps in a row

Watermark—a design pressed onto the stamp during its manufacture

Other types of interesting collectible stamp items include **tax and postage due stamps, Duck Hunting licensing stamps** (still issued today), **postal marks, souvenir pages** (first day issue stamps on a page with identifying information), and other philatelic literature such as **catalogs**.

As with rare coins, **misprints and rarities** are popular with stamp collectors. There is a lot of stamp lore and history associated with famous collectors, fakes and forgeries, and fabulous finds. The most expensive stamp in history was thought to be the **British Guiana One Cent Magenta**, found by a British twelve-year-old in 1873 among letters in his family's attic. In 1980 it was auctioned to John DuPont for $935,000. Other famous stamp rarities include the **1847 "Post Office Mauritius"**—this British colony produced only five hundred of each of its first two stamps, and erroneously marked some "Post Office" instead of "Post Paid"—and the mistakenly **inverted 1959 Canada St. Lawrence Seaway** stamp.

## AT AUCTION

In several sales during 2004 and 2005, Sotheby's auctioned "the most important collection of stamps to be sold in 50 years," that of British aristocrat and racing car driving enthusiast Sir Gawaine Baillie. One of the highest priced items, a **block of four 1840 Two Pence Blue**, sold for over $200,000. A **block of eight 1881 One Penny Lilacs** sold for 133 pounds, or around $253.

## COLLECTIONS

As with other collectibles, the more you know about the history of a collection, the better able you will be to determine its value before you approach an expert or consider its sale. Did the collector spend a lot of time on his stamps? Did he catalog things carefully, mounting the stamps in archival albums, including notes, descriptions, and literature? Are they mostly foreign or American? Is there a concentration in one or more countries? Most importantly, are most of the stamps from a period before 1935?

Many modern stamps have little or no value. Beginning stamp collectors are often advised to buy a "bucket" or packet of several hundred or even a thousand stamps to jump-start their collections. These can be had for very small amounts of money. The "starter" kits like these are used by collectors to hone their stamp research, handling, and identification skills. It's a very low-cost way to start a hobby. The wide range of prices at the Baillie auction we mentioned above also illustrate that even an important collection does not always contain exclusively rare and high-priced examples.

Some experts believe serious collectors specialize in certain areas. If you see a huge variety of stamps from all over the world, even if they are cataloged and identified, it is possible they were inexpensive to begin with and will remain that way.

If you find stamps in any condition, in an album, on envelopes, be careful not to handle them extensively. Stamp collectors use tongs. If you are going to remove any stamps from any mountings to scan or photograph them you should get a pair of your own, and ask a dealer or collector how to use them. A magnifying glass will be useful also. Do NOT try to soak any stamps to remove them from paper or envelopes.

## FIND OUT ABOUT STAMPS

*The American Philatelic Society* has one of the leading stamp collecting sites on the web, and offers an identification service as well as publications, news about shows, a stamp store, and insurance for collections. Other sites like *Stamplink* and *Find Your Stamps Value* have stamp dictionaries, advice for collectors, software, periodicals, and links to stamp museums and stamp clubs and societies.

More new online stamp identification services are cropping up every day. Some of them have free trials or, in the case of one I found, you can have one item identified and valued for $4.98 to see how it works.

Weekly and monthly stamp publications include *Linn's* (named for the famous philatelist) and *Scott's*—published by the company that also compiles and sells detailed **stamp catalogs**—are two you can investigate. Most stamps listed on eBay or traded among dealers are identified by their **Scott's catalog numbers**.

On eBay, stamps are a universe unto themselves—Stamps has its own web address, Stamps.eBay.com, its own chat room, and quick links to identification sites.

EBay also offers referrals to Stamp Trading Assistants and a site with hot tips from other sellers.

More valuable stamps can be sold through specialty dealers and auction companies.

## COMICS

Comic books have been collectible for generations, but comic collecting has boomed in recent years, especially with the popularity of films like *Spiderman* and other superhero movies and TV shows. Comics, like baseball cards, now have independent third-party grading—***Comics Guaranty Corp***, or ***CGC***, is the principal comic grading firm, and this has helped serious collectors to move into the market. Comics are graded on a numerical scale of 1 to 10, with grades above 9 considered high quality.

Comics are divided into four major historical "Ages":

### The Early Period: 1897–1937

Early comics were pulp magazine versions of newspaper comic strips. One of the first early publishers was known as National Periodical until it introduced a comic book called ***Detective Comics*** and took the name **DC**, which it still bears today.

### The Golden Age: 1938–1955

The **Golden Age** is considered to have begun with the first *Superman* comic, published by DC Comics, and dominated by other DC superheroes such as **Batman, Green Lantern, Wonder Woman, The Flash**, and **Hawkman; Fawcett**'s Captain Marvel; **Marvel Comics**' Captain America; and the **Archie** series.

### The Silver Age: 1956–1969

The **Silver Age** is thought to have begun with **DC**'s modernized versions of *Flash* and *Green Lantern* and the *Justice League of America*; and **Marvel**'s *Spiderman, Fantastic Four, Incredible Hulk, Iron Man, X-Men,* and *Avengers*.

### The Modern Age: 1970s–1980s

The **Modern Age**, which some collectors call the **Bronze Age**, is the era of the miniseries and antiheroes, horror and fantasy with such titles as **DC**'s

*Batman: The Dark Night Returns*, *Swamp Thing*, *Crisis on Infinite Earths*, and its **Vertigo** line of more "adult" themes.

There is a lot of history associated with all these periods, mostly concerning the artists and executives that ran the comic companies and shaped their creative output.

---

## AT AUCTION

In October 2002 actor Nicholas Cage auctioned his comic collection at Heritage Galleries for nearly $1.7 million. Some highlights were a **1940 Detective #38**, featuring the first appearance of Batman's sidekick, Robin, which sold for $120,750, and a **1963 Spider-Man #1**, which brought $70,150.

In January 2006, Heritage auctioned a **Captain America #1** graded 9.0 for over $96,000.

---

## FIND OUT ABOUT COMICS

***The Official Overstreet Comic Book Price Guide*** is considered the "bible" to comic identification, and there is now an Overstreet guide to grading comics. You can check comics in the guide alphabetically, by issue number and title. If you can't find the information on the cover of the comic book, check the copyright page, usually inside the front cover, for the **"indicia"** (date, title, issue number). If you monitor listings on eBay (comics are in the Collectibles category) you will notice the CGC grades in descriptions and that some sellers reference the Overstreet catalog values.

If you have questions about comic identification and values, or are trying to find out if you should have a comic graded, you can use the **community message boards** on CGC's website to ask questions, or try to find an expert on the eBay forums.

## PHOTOGRAPHS

Photography is gaining importance as a collectible asset. Works by important pioneers of photographic art such as **Edward Weston, Alfred Stieglitz, Dorothea Lange, Edward Steichen,** and the popular **Ansel Adams** have been in demand for some time. Other more contemporary photograph artists include **William Eggleston, Helmet Newton, Langdon Coburn,** and **Robert Mapplethorpe**.

---

## AT AUCTION

A rare 1904 photo of a moonlit pond by **Edward Steichen** sold for $2.9 million at Sotheby's in February 2006, breaking a world record for any photograph at auction. A 2003 museum exhibition of the works of influential American photographer **Diane Arbus** caused a spike in her prices; her famous piece, "**Identical Twins,**" sold at Sotheby's April 2004 photography sale for $478,000. At the same sale, a 1936 photo of a segregated barbershop in Atlanta by **Walker Evans**, famous for his Depression-era farm and urban scenes, sold for $198,400

---

The work of some commercially successful photographers such as fashion icon Richard Avedon, who died in 2004, **Cecil Beaton, Irving Penn,** and **Alfred Einsenstadt** is also gaining interest among collectors.

**Historical** photographs may be categorized as memorabilia, historical, entertainment, or sports collectibles. Vintage photos and albums can often bring interesting prices on eBay. Photos of all types from the turn of the century through the twenties and thirties seem to sell well—a collection of eight original photos of Buffalo Bill and his Wild West Show tour of France in 1905 brought $980. A selection of five **Farm Security Administration** vintage pieces from 1930s Appalachia sold for over $1900, and two 1920s photos of Buddhist monks in Ceylon brought $580. Even some ordinary vintage photo albums have sold anywhere from $25 to several hundred dollars. World War II is also an area of particular interest.

Many local libraries and historical societies maintain photographic collections and might be able to give you assistance in identifying photographs.

## SCRIPOPHILY—WHAT'S THAT?

Most of us have never heard of "**Scripophily**." This odd word refers to the *study of old paper articles*, everything from defunct stock certificates, outdated paper money, government and war bonds, bank drafts and demand notes, deeds, mineral rights and other legal papers, letters, maps, and just about anything else on old paper that you could think of.

## ABOUT STOCKS

If you find stock certificates, or anything that looks like a financial instrument, you can make photocopies of them and show them to a stockbroker, who can have them researched by a stock brokerage firm. All major brokerage houses have departments that can trace the history of old certificates and tell you whether or not they are still valid. Just because a company is not in business anymore does not always mean the stock is worthless—companies are frequently bought out by other companies, and holders of the original shares are sometimes entitled to cash or shares in the acquiring company.

If you don't have a broker, or just want to try this on your own, there are two major directories you can find at the public library:

*Directory of Obsolete Securities*—published by Financial Information, Inc., Jersey City, New Jersey

*Robert D. Fisher Manual of Valuable and Worthless Securities*—published by ***R.M. Smythe & Co., Inc.***

Smythe also has an online search service, and there's also a site called **Stock Search International**. Both of these charge fees for research; Stock Search also has a database you can purchase.

Other types of documents can be researched at historical societies and by specialists at major auction companies.

## CURRENCY AND BANKNOTES

In 2003, a collection of unused banknotes from the 1800s, stored in a bank vault on the East Coast and virtually untouched for more than a hundred years, was found and sold to collectors for an aggregate value of over $10 million. The original face value of the money was $20,000! Some, but not all, coin dealers also specialize in paper currency.

***Scripophily.Com, Sammler's***, and ***Banknotes.Com*** are all interesting sites that deal in old currency, defunct bank drafts, bonds, and other paper monetary items. There are price guides on this subject, many of them published by Krause, such as the *Standard Catalog of U.S. Paper Money* by Charles Krause and *The Standard Catalog of World Paper Money* by George S. Cuhaj.

The *Professional Currency Dealers Association* also has informational booklets and lists of member dealers.

## POSTCARDS

Postcards and to a lesser extent greeting cards are a popular subarea in the paper assets category.

Postcards are thought to have originated around the 1860s; early examples with original photographs or chromolithographs are among the most valuable. An original, unused card from around 1900 featuring a lithograph by the French Art Nouveau illustrator **Alphonse Mucha** sold recently on eBay for over $1500.

Military cards especially from the early 1900s and World War II are also desirable.

Postcard collectors can be fairly passionate. In 1999, the University of Texas exhibited a historical collection donated by Fort Worth businessman and civic leader Jenkins Garrett, who had accumulated over thirteen thousand cards, many of them documenting early Texas history and scenery.

The *Postcard Traders Association* is a British collecting club whose website includes ads, events, research, and buying and selling resources. *San Francisco Bay Area Postcard Club* has a similar site with a list of research and identification links.

## MAGAZINES

The market for back issues of magazines is large and active, but it can be fickle. Recently on eBay, a 1955 copy of *Life Magazine* with Ernest Hemingway on the cover wasn't selling, but a 1961 copy with Mickey Mantle and Roger Maris of the New York Yankees (baseball again!) was selling for $86.

A beautiful-looking selection of antique *Harper's Bazaar* magazines from 1886, with lots of vintage fashions and ads, was not attracting any interest, but a 1988 issue of *Harper's Bazaar* Spanish issue with **Madonna** on the cover was getting lots of action; the bid was over $100 with more than three days to go!

My friend A. J., the eBay trading assistant, reports that some of the desirable names in magazines are *Playboy*, *National Lampoon*, *MAD*, *OZ*, and *Circus* (counterculture/rock magazines from the sixties); *Punk* and *Slash* (punk rock magazines from the eighties); *Rolling Stone*, *Heavy Metal*, and magazines of sports and military interest.

Some vintage teen celebrity and Beatles magazines sell well, as well as martial arts publications and men's magazines such as *Argosy* and *Rogue*. Early literary magazines and journals and some of the "underground" newspapers of the 1960s are gaining collector interest.

Age is not necessarily the important ingredient for value—popularity counts in this category. In browsing eBay on an ordinary day, I saw some interesting vintage 1930s movie magazines with Jean Harlow and Joan Crawford covers going for around $35, less than a 1967 copy of *Newsweek* with "it-girl" model Twiggy on the cover ($50). A July 1957 issue of *Life* with then-Senator John F. Kennedy was selling for only $6; a year (1944) of twelve model train magazines was briskly bid at over $25. A lot of the twelve 1927 issues of *American Boy* magazine was also getting some interest at over $27.

The first issue of *Playboy*, from December 1953, featuring Marilyn Monroe, is a collector's item that sells for several thousand dollars. The 1950s *Playboys* are generally the most sought-after—after the fifties, values decline to a few dollars per copy, with a few issues, such as those featuring Farah Fawcett or other famous celebrities, going a bit higher.

A contribution by a famous artist or author can also add value—a December 1910 issue of *Ladies' World* featuring a short story by *Wizard of Oz* author **L. Frank Baum** sold for over $140, and an **Arthur Conan Doyle** Sherlock Holmes story in an otherwise unremarkable 1912 copy of *The World* magazine caused the price to go over $120.

Early sports magazines such as *Harley Davidson*, *Hot Rod*, *Forza* (Ferrari), and *Yachting* also sell well in years or larger collections. Early *National Geographic*s and *Good Housekeeping*s are collectible, but these two started publication before 1900, so only the earliest are considered rare.

Older "pulp" sci-fi magazines sell well, as do vintage issues of *Analog* and *Isaac Asimov* magazines.

Magazines may not be big-ticket items but they are ideal eBay items—fun, easy to pack, and inexpensive to ship, since you can take advantage of Media Mail postage rates. Check them carefully to make sure all the pages are intact, that nothing has been cut out or removed. A magazine without a subscription mailing label will generally be more valuable.

Remember with all paper assets that small flaws in condition may dramatically reduce value. When you catalog your items, make notes of any tears, soiling, edgewear, pencil marks, folds or creases, and spots or stains, and remember to note the defects in your descriptions if you offer any items for sale.

# 14

# ART, RUGS, SILVER, AND COLLECTIBLES

O n the wall, on the floor, in drawers, and in curio cabinets—some of the objects we see every day are the ones we might forget to ask questions about!

## FINE ART

Art has been collected and prized for centuries. Possibly no other asset fascinates and stimulates the collector and the marketplace to such an extent.

"Fine Art" is generally considered to be *painting, drawing; other works on paper such as watercolor, gouache, or pastel; sculpture; and original prints* on paper (also called "graphics") such as woodcuts, lithographs, etchings, and seriographs. The term "original" with respect to prints means that the artist creates the design on a plate or block and a **limited edition** of copies of the design is produced, so a print can be an "original" and not be one of a kind.

Fine art **reproductions** are also very popular today, and can include posters, copies of original prints, *giclees* (reproductions on canvas), and hand-painted oil reproductions.

Lately, fine art auctions have also included photographs, animation cels, light sculptures, and paintings produced by chimpanzees and elephants! *Yes, really!*

There are many diverse types of collectible art. There is the world of major galleries, museums, and collections, the styles that are representative of important historical movements. **"Listed artist"** is a term some dealers, appraisers, and art experts use to refer to an artist who is mentioned in art history reference books, or whose work has auction records.

Many fine local and regional artists have prestigious gallery shows and collector patronage. Some commercially popular and decorative artists have huge followings and command impressive prices.

## HOW TO FIND OUT ABOUT ART

Until recently, information about art prices and values was only accessible to profesionals in the art world. Catalogs of the works of many artists exist, but they are often expensive and difficult to obtain. Auction results would become available weeks or months after a sale.

In recent years, though, several important and indispensable internet sites for art values and information have emerged, and are used by professionals and collectors alike. **ArtNet, ArtPrice, AskArt,** and **ArtFact** all have free and subscription access to literally millions of art sales records, and offer information resources and dealer referrals as well. ArtFact will give you a broad range of prices for an artist without subscribing. On ArtNet you can also easily access a list of dealers and galleries that represent particular artists and styles. AskArt (The American Artists Bluebook) has a directory of 42,000 artists, a research center, art glossary and art marketplace where you can buy and sell.

These sites will not turn you into an instant art appraiser! But they are likely to provide you with useful information about artists and comparable works you may own. You can often see examples of an artist's work and find out if the artist is exhibited in museums, has auction records, or is mentioned in reference books. You can obtain referrals to dealers. Galleries may help you identify a piece, purchase or consign works of art from you, give you information about the market for your art, and refer you to experts and appraisers if you need one.

## IS IT VALUABLE?

If you have a piece of art you feel is worth evaluating, you can bring a piece to a free appraisal day at a local auction gallery, or email photos to the art staff of a major or regional auction house. They may give you a ballpark auction estimate, or if they feel you have a piece which needs further evaluation, they may refer you to an outside expert with knowledge of a particular artist or school.

You can ask at a local university if someone in the art history department is willing or qualified to look at your pieces to give you assistance in identifications. A museum may have an available curator or other staff person who is allowed to give you some kind of opinion on identification only—art museums usually do not get involved in discussions of value or perform appraisals, but they may refer you to someone who can. The art critic for your local newspaper may be familiar with local dealers in the area and the types of work they sell; the public library should have an art reference section.

**Art values** are based on price history at auction and in galleries, and many other factors, including the importance and popularity of an artist, and the qualities of a piece. **Unsigned** works can be difficult to evaluate. Even if they are old, and belong to a specific school, they may not attract the kind of investor who will pay high prices. **Antique paintings** from the eighteenth to early twentieth century can have a very wide range of values, from a few hundred dollars into the many tens of thousands, depending on the artist, or if it is especially representative of a particular school. **Old Master paintings**, from the fourteenth to the early eighteenth century, while generally considered valuable, are often problematic to identify and authenticate, and prices can sometimes be unexpectedly reasonable.

There are some excellent fine art price guides, especially *Davenport's Fine Art Price Guide* (published by Gordon's Art Reference)—considered the "gold standard" for information on art values. *Hislop's Official*

*International Price Guide to Fine Art* (House of Collectibles) has some excellent introductory materials about the art market, condition, and advice about auctions. There are also fine art bibliographic reference books such as *The Fine Art Index* (International Art Reference) where you can find lists of books and catalogues about your area of interest.

## ANTIQUITIES

**Antiquities** is a general term for objects of archeological interest—ancient sculptures, statues, pottery, masks, and other objects. The marketplace is relatively small and highly specialized; the major auction houses, for instance, may each only conduct a couple of antiquities sales a year, as opposed to twenty-five or thirty jewelry or art sales.

Since 1970, a date established by the **UNESCO Convention on Cultural Property**, the sale and exportation of antiquities from most foreign countries has been regulated by both international law and individual nations. The laws came into being largely to protect against looting and illicit trafficking. Legitimate purchases by collectors and museums can still go on, as long as the objects have been known to be in documented collections.

Some experts today feel the antiquities market may be undervalued, partly because of the complexities involved. In some countries, an object can actually be considered "illicit" or illegal to purchase if proof of ownership under applicable law cannot be provided.

Private collections formed in the early part of the twentieth century can and do contain valuable pieces. But reproductions of all types of ancient objects abound, and can be found all over the world in gift shops, decorator salons, arts and crafts fairs, museum shops, in tourist meccas, and even in antique shops.

A local dealer, museum, or archeology or ancient art department at a university may be able to assist you in determining the age and origin of objects you might have. Any history or documentation about the piece will prove invaluable in helping to determine its age. You can take digital photos of any artifacts and email them along with a description (size, material, identifying characteristics) to an antiquities expert at one of the major auction houses and get a no-obligation reading on whether the piece might merit further evaluation. A local historical society may also be able to give you a referral to an antiquities authority.

Antiquities resources on the web are still emerging. Many commercial websites advertising antiquities actually offer reproductions. You can check out library resources to look for reference guides. *The AACA, Authentic Artifact Collector Association* is a group dedicated to Native American Indian relics and artifacts. The *International Association of Dealers in Ancient Art* has a website with links to member galleries.


## SILVER, COPPER, AND BRASS

Many people have some type of silver, especially dinnerware or tea services. Most silver is hallmarked except for some very early pieces, making identification easier than with some other types of antiques. Because silver flatware, tea services, and similar items have been produced in considerable quantity and continue to be manufactured today, many very nice pieces from recent decades may sell for less than new ones. Some favorite patterns do well; vintage sets of **Gorham Chantilly** flatware routinely sell on eBay for $1–3000, depending on the size. Monogrammed silver is considered less desirable for resale. Other popular manufacturers include **Wallace**, **Whiting**, **Lunt**, **Reed & Barton**, **International**, **Rogers**, and **Towle**.

The term "sterling" was used on American silver after 1860. American sterling is marked with the word "sterling" or the numbers 925/1000. Pre-1860 pieces, sometimes referred to as "coin silver," bear the initials or name of the manufacturer or silversmith. However, more modern silverplate also bears the name of its manufacturer, and may or may NOT include the words "plate" or "A1."

True **early American silver** is valuable and rare; many colonial pieces are in museums, and items such as teapots from the early 1800s can sell for several thousand dollars. Other important silver includes **Tiffany** and **George Jensen**, a Danish silversmith who founded his company in 1904 and gained popularity during the twenties and thirties through the fifties.

## AT AUCTION

A sugar bowl made by **Paul Revere** as a wedding gift in 1762 sold for $232,000 at Sotheby's January 2004 Americana auction. A **George Jensen "Blossom"** pattern flatware service surged past its $20–30,000 estimate and sold for $180,000 at Christie's January 2005 silver sale.

British silver has been hallmarked since the 1300s. "**Sheffield Plate**" is a kind of antique English silverplate process using a thin layer of silver coated over copper. Sheffield Plate originated around 1760, so older pieces can have value. Sometimes Sheffield can be identified by a pinkish tinge caused by areas of the silver wearing thin.

The study of silver marks, particularly that of antique English silver, is an area to which experts have devoted lifetimes. You can find an online encyclopedia or website such as *Replacements* or *The Online Silver Encyclopedia (925-1000)*, which has pattern and mark identification service. You can also post a question and a photo on a discussion forum if you need help deciphering a mark.

Always clean dust and dirt from silver before polishing—dust can scratch the surface if it is rubbed with polish. You can wash silver in warm water and a mild soap but avoid soaking it in water for any length of time. Don't wash it in the dishwasher. A nonabrasive commercial silver polish like Goddard's should be safe for most antique pieces. Stay away from harsh silver "dips," which can actually strip the patina. A polishing cloth can help restore luster and shine. Don't try to remove or reshape any dents by yourself—a valuable piece that needs repair or restoration should be evaluated by a silversmith.

**Stainless steel flatware** is becoming surprisingly collectible. My friend, A. J., the eBay trading assistant, recently sold several **Lauffer Bedford** five-piece Modern style place settings from the sixties for $50 apiece. A sixty-nine-piece **George Jensen** Danish Modern set sold for $715. Ornate styles also are in demand—an **Oneida Frederick II** twelve-piece set with serving pieces brought $760.

**Copper** was used to make decorative objects in the Arts and Crafts period, notably at the Roycroft community. Some pieces were characterized by hand-hammering and special finishes. Roycroft copper was made from 1906 into the 1920s, and most pieces are marked with an orb-and-cross design incorporating the letter "R." Modern decorative copper is protected by a lacquer coating and won't tarnish. **Bronze** (an alloy of copper and tin) was popularly utilized in the Art Nouveau period; Tiffany modeled his lamp bases in bronze. Other popular bronze items of the period were small sculptures, inkwells, desk accessories, vases, and candlesticks.

Antique metal objects made of copper and brass need to be cleaned with special nonabrasive polishes intended for use specifically on those metals.

Pewter (an alloy of tin and lead) does not tarnish, but it is porous and may scratch or chip. Pewter and bronze should not require much cleaning; they can be dusted or polished with a cloth.

Identification and value price guides (such as Maryanne Dolan's *American Sterling Silver Flatware, 1830's–1990's,* from Krause) are plentiful for silver, copper, and brass items.

## RUGS

Heavy and cumbersome as they may be to lug over to your neighborhood carpet store to get an expert ID, some rugs are definitely worth more than their weight in dollars. By the way, a **"rug"** is something under 2 meters or approximately 6 1/2 feet in length—small enough to hang on a wall. Anything larger is referred to as a **"carpet."** Both words are used colloquially when discussing the marketplace.

**"Oriental" rug** is a general term referring to a carpet made of hand-knotted sheep's or lamb's wool, made in a variety of countries on the Asian continent. The greater number of knots per square inch, the higher the quality—a superb rug may have five hundred to a thousand knots per square inch.

The important categories of Oriental rugs include **Persian**, or Iranian, which are generally classified by the regions in which they are made—**Tabriz** is one of the major regions, others include **Sarouk**, **Kashan**, **Heriz**, **Sarapi**, **Isfahan**, and **Kerman**. Persian rugs are further classified by the design or pattern they display; an expert can usually tell the origin of a Persian carpet by its pattern and subpatterns, and also by the structure of the knots. The materials, the "selvage" (finishing of the edge) and the colors will also give him information as to age and origin. Persian rugs can be tribal or rural, as well as made in urban centers.

Other types of important rugs include **Bokhara** and **Turkoman**, both made in Pakistan; **Turkish**, **Chinese**, **Caucasian**, **Indian**, and **Tibetan**; **American Indian** rugs such as Navajo; and French **Aubusson** carpets. "Savonnerie" refers to a style of knotted weave begun in France in the 1700s to emulate Oriental style, and still made today all over the world.

Persian rugs became scarce in the 1980s and 1990s as a result of a U.S. trade embargo against Iran; consequently many older examples have appreciated considerably in value. Decorative Persian "type" or design rugs, available in large quantities from carpet stores, are basically copies of whatever Persian style they emulate. Most of these are not actually made in Iran, and even if made by hand are not considered collectible items. Some rug experts advise viewing an authentic carpet next to an imitation to look for variances in knot count, vividness of colors, sharpness of design, and other elements of quality. Value in rugs follows the same rules as for other types of collectibles: rarity, quality, craftsmanship, and excellence of design.

---

### AT AUCTION

Skinner's, Sotheby's, and Christie's hold carpet auctions, and many other houses include them in estate and combination sales. A late-seventeenth- early-eighteenth-century **Moghul millefleur carpet** from the Vanderbilt mansion in New York City sold at Christie's for $992,500 at an April 1995 sale.

---

More typical prices lately have ranged from the $7–8000 to the $20–40,000 area. Potentially valuable rugs, especially anything over fifty years old, need to be authenticated simply because the imitation market is so large. You can try a local rug dealer for a preliminary evaluation, but it is best to find a rug expert at a major auction house and email them some information with photos.

Fortunately many rugs have durability and can be used and enjoyed. If yours do not turn out to be valuable, they may still be salable as decorator items or donated.

## COLLECTIBLES

The word "**Collectibles**" really has two meanings, though it is used to describe thousands of things! One meaning is a catch-all for any kind of tangible asset, things that are accumulated in collections. The other meaning is for a class of small decorative or fun object, *not necessarily old or valuable.*

Some collectibles fit into other categories like toys, small antiques, or memorabilia; but others are modern gift type items, or, well—just things that might seem useless or unimportant to one person, but treasured and valued by someone else.

It is literally amazing how many different types of objects are collected!

Fishing lures and reels
Pens, inkwells, and other writing accessories
Quilts
Cigarette lighters, pipes, ashtrays, and other smoking memorabilia
Scraps (a term for cutout pieces of greeting cards and cardboard adver-
    tisements)
Yo-yos
Knives
Ties
Thimbles and other sewing accessories
Bubble Bath containers
Lunch Boxes
Corkscrews, bottle openers, and other beverage-related accessories
Boxes, including wooden, porcelain, leather, enamel, and metal
Paperweights
Famous animal figurines
Music Boxes
Snow Domes
Marbles
Cameras

Canes
Early industrial equipment parts
Vintage radios and TVs
Vintage kitchen appliances
Crayola materials
Old photographs and albums
Campbell's Soup memorabilia
African American folk art figure dolls
Zeppelin and other ballooning memorabilia
Salt and pepper shakers
Scrimshaw
Antique phonographs
Door knobs and door stops
Letter openers
Clocks
Perfume Bottles
Hatpins
Padlocks
Bottles
Calendars
Buttons

Many of these collectible areas have their own price guides, collector clubs, and organizations, and sometimes entire shows are devoted to them. Others are smaller areas of interest, usually classified with memorabilia or small antiques.

A few words about some of the most "widely held" in the small collectibles universe:

## COLLECTIBLE FIGURINES

There is good news and bad news about **collectible figurines**. The marketplace is enormous. This means (the good news) there is a wealth of information resources—collector clubs, price guides, newsletters, online retailers, and informational websites. It also means (the bad news) that supply is plentiful, and "real world" prices are often far below many of those quoted in price guides. Still, there is a devoted collector market for figurines, and some particular pieces that are sought-after can achieve their price-guide values or more.

Figurines have been popular for several hundred years. The **Meissen** porcelain companies in Germany under the artistry of **Johann Kandler** at the **Royal Saxon Porcelain factory** popularized figurines in the early 1700s, and many pieces that actually date from that period are in museum collections. In the nineteenth century the Meissen styles enjoyed popularity and were extensively reproduced. British potters also fashioned decorative figures from the 1700s; animal figurines produced at factories in the Staffordshire area of England in the mid- and late-nineteenth century caught on with collectors of the day, and are still reproduced today.

The "boom" in figurines is really a twentieth-century phenomenon. In 1935 the **Goebel** porcelain company introduced the first figurines based on artwork by Franciscan **Sister Maria Innocenta Hummel**, an artist who had studied at Munich's Academy of Applied Arts. Hummel's popular drawings of country children had already been reproduced as postcards. The Goebel figurines were an instant hit at the 1935 Leipzig Fair. Hummel continued to design figurines for Goebel until her early death from tuberculosis in 1946. Goebel continues to manufacture Hummel designs, called M. I. Hummel, to this day.

The "**Dresden**" style of porcelain is more an artistic movement than a particular manufacturer. Four different manufacturers in the German city registered a blue crown Dresden mark in 1883. The Dresden style of figurines often featured a technique of dipping real crinoline lace in liquid porcelain, and the dainty figures are most often seen portraying courtly life, playing instruments or dancing to show off their petticoats. Some German Dresden porcelain is referred to as "Irish" Dresden. Put that one on your list of collectibles with confusing names!

Figurines were first made by **Royal Doulton** in 1913 and popularized by a visit by then-Queen Mary to the factory. Since then over three thousand different Royal Doulton figurines have been manufactured. You can take a tour of the factory (still in operation) near Stoke-on-Trent, England.

Modern figurines abound today, produced by hundreds of manufacturers. Some online retailers have over twenty thousand items each and there are more than that number on eBay every day. A few (and I do mean *very* few) of the names are **Royal Worcester, Boehm, Guiseppe Armani, Precious Moments, Beatrix Potter, Lenox, Swarovski, Flambro, Franklin Mint, Danbury Mint,** and **Balint Kramlik. Disney Studios** manufactures modern porcelain Disney collectibles. **Lladro** (pronounced "Ya-DRO") porcelains are manufactured in Valencia, Spain, and known for delicacy and quality.

For most figurines it is easy to find a price guide. If you don't know the manufacturer, take one to an antique mall or a collectibles show, or send a photo to an online message board on a collectibles portal such as *World Collectors Net* and you'll probably receive a helpful reply. If you want to comparison shop for prices, visit one of the multitude of online retailers or browse items on eBay using the search word "figurine." Most of them are listed under the "Decorative Collectibles" category but you can also find them under Disneyana, Dolls and Bears, and Animal Collectibles.

## PENS

Do not, do *not* toss out those old pens in Dad's desk before you look them over. Collectors of writing instruments are very dedicated and passionate. Even antique "nibs"—the engraved gold tips of antique fountain pens— might command several hundred dollars to the right collector. **Pentrace** is an online pen collecting community with bulletin boards, classified ads, news of shows, and other resources. Or check out a dealer site such as the **Vintage Pen Website** to see examples of pens for sale, everything from famous pens used to sign historical documents to vintage **Parkers, Sheaffers,** and **Watermans** from the early twentieth century, many retailing from the low hundreds to well over a thousand dollars.

## PINS

Pin collecting is a modern phenomenon, although souvenir pins of all kinds have been around for ages. Possibly the modern era of pin collecting began in the 1980s, first at the **Lake Placid Winter Olympics** in 1980 and then the **1984 Los Angeles Olympics**. Pins, originally used as badges, were around at the very first modern Olympics in Athens in 1896. Originally they were given to the athletes, who exchanged them as mementos and tokens of friendship. Companies such as Budweiser and Coca Cola helped to popularize Olympic pin trading.

Today some of the most collectible pins are from **Disney, Nascar, Coca Cola, Star Wars, sports teams and events**, and the **Hard Rock Cafe**. Some of the more valuable Hard Rock pins include those issued to staff for openings and other events, famous guitars, and limited edition celebrity models. Prices of desirable Hard Rock pins can run from $100 to over $400—*yes, really!*

## LUNCH BOXES

The "Holy Grail" of vintage collectible lunch boxes (yes, those colorful tin containers kids lugged to school in the fifties and sixties) is the 1954 **Superman** model made by **Adco Liberty**. An absentee bidder purchased one at Skinner's in March 2000, for $11,500. That record was shattered in July 2004, when another sold to collector Joseph Soucy for $13,000!

Other desirables include **Aladdin**'s Hopalong Cassidy and Roy Rogers models—first introduced in the early 1950s—and **The Beatles**—a 1965 light blue box featuring the four mop tops sold recently on eBay for $800. Popular sixties TV show models featuring **The Jetsons, Star Trek, Beverly Hillbillies, The Monkees, Batman,** and others sell in the $2–400 range.

Value is increased if the original thermos and cup are present; the lunchbox also needs to have its original handle. Remember, as with toys, these will not be particularly desirable to collectors if rusted, dented, or in otherwise subpar condition.

## BEANIE BABIES

In 1993 **Beanie Babies** burst on the scene creating one of the most memorable collectible "bubbles" in modern history. They were the creation of a toy salesman turned entrepreneur named H. Ty Warner. His toy company, *Ty*, will certainly go down in marketing history. Beanies were cute little soft animal toys stuffed with beans. There were nine original animal characters including Patti the Platypus and Cubbi the Bear, and they came with red heart-shaped tags. Within a few years Beanies had attracted a collector frenzy, and a number of other "look-alike" toys were produced by other companies. In 1997, some Beanie prices were soaring to over a thousand dollars apiece, and Ty's sales exceeded $1 billion.

Rare, early Beanies can still be worth a thousand dollars or more, but the market is selective today. Some Beanies can be dated by their tags and there are specialist dealers who offer authentication services. Prices in the low-to-mid hundreds are more common for some of the earlier models especially with tags and packaging. But realize that Beanies are still being manufactured, and many Beanies out there have little resale value. Just check some of the over seventy thousand eBay listings and you'll get the picture. Ty's website has a message board where you can post or browse ads to buy and sell Beanies. Several sites offer identification and authentication services.

## BEARS

Modern collectible bears are generally less pricey than the antique Teddy Bears we discussed in chapter 10, but collectors are devoted to them, and the market is still growing.

**Knickerbocker** toys won the license for Smokey the Bear in the 1960s and also marketed the popular TV character, Yogi Bear. Vintage Knickerbocker bears can range from $20 to the hundreds, and can be identified and dated by their labels.

**Care Bears** were introduced in the 1980s by **American Greetings**, using the artwork of Elena Kucharik. **Kenner** began producing the toys in 1985, and the bears became instant celebrities with a TV series and three animated films. The Care Bears are enjoying a revival in 2005, after a DVD and a new movie, so the prices of the 1980s toys have been on the rise. Collectible Care Bears can sell in the $50–80 range.

**Boyd's** is another brand of collectible bears. The toy company, begun in 1979 by G. M. Lowenthal and his wife, Justina Unger, originally produced reproductions of antique duck decoys, and started branching out into plush and later resin bears in the early 1980s. Some of the more valuable "retired" or discontinued Boyd's Bears sell for two or three hundred dollars. Boyd's is still in production today, so the supply of contemporary bears is plentiful.

**Starbuck's** has even been getting into the "bear" game recently too with its line of "Bearista" bears. I saw a "Summer Beach Girl" Bearista model from 2002 sell for $178 on eBay. The **ValContemporary** bear artists are also turning out pricey designer "art bears," some made of exotic fur, others with designer costumes or other accessories.

## WHAT TO DO WITH THEM ALL

With all collectibles, both vintage and modern, follow a few basic steps:

- Look for a price and identification guide with some information about the marketplace
- Go over each item for identifying marks and tags
- Check eBay listings for comparable items
- Conduct a web search for collectors' clubs or informational sites
- Search eBay forums for previous questions
- Visit an antique mall or show to get pricing ideas
- Contact the manufacturer if currently in business and ask for historical information

*Selling Tip*: Popular collectibles are also sorted on eBay by **keywords**. You can type a keyword, such as "bear," or search alphabetically. If you click on a letter under keywords, you'll see some of the most common collectibles on eBay starting with that letter: for example, "D" has Disney, Depression Glass, Darth Vader. Often eBay will feature the most popular searches under a category as well. These are all ways to browse and see as many items as you can, without having to be more specific about an item you may be trying to identify.

# 15

# AUCTIONS, ESTATE SALES, AND DEALERS

The work involved in identifying your collectibles has an important payoff. The more information you have, the more you will be able to find the best outlet if you want to sell a piece or collection. An item that has been identified and then is placed in the right selling environment has the best chance of realizing the most value.

What's the best place to sell your collectible? Let's take a look at some options:

## SELLING AT AUCTION

For many, an auction might seem like a distant land, accessible only to dealers and experts, or the wealthy and important. The truth is, auction companies of all sizes are right around the corner from us all. Not only that, but the staff people at the very largest and most important auction houses are also accessible, and very interested in what you may have to sell.

What exactly is an auction, and how do we get our valuables into one? An auction is a **public sale** in which property or merchandise is sold to the

**highest bidder**. All sorts of items are routinely sold at auctions every day. Besides *antiques, art, and other valuables, real estate, livestock, and industrial equipment* are some of the most common kinds of property regularly sold at auctions. In small towns and rural communities, you might find an auction company that deals in all of these!

Sometimes a federal or state government agency or local police department will auction seized, abandoned, or tax-defaulted property. The GSA, or General Services Administration, frequently auctions surplus government property.

There are some technically different formats for auctions, but the most common for selling physical property is the **single-item, rising price** type of auction, where increasingly higher bids are accepted until there is no higher price offered. The item is considered "sold" at the last, highest bid.

## INTERNATIONAL AUCTION COMPANIES

*Sotheby's* and *Christie's* are the world's two largest international fine art auction companies that operate in the United States. Based in New York and London, the two companies also conduct their auctions in major art capitals of the world—Geneva, Paris, Rome, Zurich, Milan—and in other cities such as Amsterdam, Hong Kong, Madrid, Munich, and St. Moritz.

Both companies also have field offices, or "associate" offices, in major cities throughout the United States. These offices are for the purpose of contact with the public. You can get in touch with a field office to have items evaluated, and discuss possibilities for placing your items in an auction, or you can correspond directly with the New York office to get an idea if your item is suitable for an auction.

Sotheby's and Christie's together represent more than one-third of the art and antiques auction business in the world, each company achieving auction sale revenues in 2005 of close to $3 billion. Both companies have a history that dates back to the 1700s, and both were started in London. Christie's began in 1766, auctioning fine art to the elite of Georgian society. Sotheby's had its origins in 1744, initially as an auctioneer of rare books. One of their first "important sales" was Napoleon's personal library. Today both companies auction a wide range of items. Besides traditional antiques, fine art, jewelry, stamps, and coins, specialist areas include: wine, automobiles, photographs, musical instruments, antiquities, sporting guns, memorabilia, animation and comic art, Russian icons, clocks and mechanical music instruments, folk art, garden statuary, carpets, teddy bears, and even cigars!

## HOW MUCH DOES IT HAVE TO BE WORTH?

How valuable does something have to be to sell at Sotheby's or Christie's?

It depends on what kind of an item it is. An item in an auction is referred to as a "lot," and each department generally has a minimum lot value for an item accepted into a sale. But this depends on the sale and also on the type of item. In a wine, book, or stamp auction, it is common to see some prices for items sold in the low hundreds. In a jewelry or art auction, pieces may range from a thousand dollars up to many hundreds of thousands.

An **average** lot size at a house like Sotheby's or Christie's might be close to $10,000, but that takes into account that some items that sell in the hundreds of thousands, while some sell for a few hundred. Each category will have a target or estimated minimum lot value, but this may be flexible.

The specialists on the staff of these companies look at furniture, jewels, decorative art objects, paintings, and other property to evaluate the probable value of these items at auction. They visit the homes of people who have collections, or review digital photos and details that pour in from around the country and the world.

Experts on the staff of major auction houses watch markets and follow the trends of collectors. An item either will or won't be suitable for the type of major sale that attracts high-net-worth investors from all over the world. This decision won't be based solely on the dollar value of the item—as we've learned, *rarity, scarcity, quality, and popularity* will all add to the equation. The staff at Sotheby's and Christie's evaluate sale results from all over the world. They know what museums are exhibiting, what major investors are purchasing, and what major pieces may be coming up for sale that could influence prices.

In other words, there may be no special dollar amount or particular attribute that will "qualify" an item for a Sotheby's or Christie's sale.

Sometimes it will come down to—what are high-end collectors interested in buying, and how well does an item fit with current market demand?

At the major houses, an item that is evaluated is given an **"estimate,"** which is the probable price range the item should sell for. The estimate is based on prior sales of comparable items, or what the piece is likely to sell for. Many times a piece will sell for a price significantly higher or lower than its estimate, but the estimate is a guideline for both bidder and seller. It can help someone who is listing an item for sale establish a **reserve price**, or a minimum guaranteed price below which the item cannot be sold.

You can get in touch with Sotheby's and Christie's by phone, by mail, or by email. Both companies will respond to inquiries with photos. You can visit their websites, view catalogs, browse completed auction results, look at the sale calendars, and most of all get familiar with the types of sales they conduct. Contact them if you have:

- important collections, older antiques, jewelry with valuable stones
- pieces that are signed or have a provenance
- pieces that you or your appraiser believe to be valuable and warrant more expert evaluation

The major auction companies welcome inquiries from people with all sorts of items and collections. They know it is just as possible to stumble across a rare item as it is an ordinary one. If your item is not of the caliber for one of their sales, they may suggest you contact a smaller or more specialized auction company to get an evaluation of your item.

## SPECIALIZED, REGIONAL, AND LOCAL

Many other smaller, fine-quality auction companies, some of which have areas of specialty, are located in large cities. *Swann Galleries* in New York is known for sales of rare books, manuscripts, maps, and other works on paper; *Stack's* specializes in rare coins. *Doyle's*, another New York company, and *Skinner's* in Boston both have a strong focus on furniture, decorative art, and fine art and jewelry. *Bonham's* is another auction firm that started in London in the late 1700s, and still has headquarters there. In 2002 Bonham's acquired *Butterfield's*, a San Francisco–based company with offices in Los

Angeles, creating a strong combination of international and regional expertise. *Heritage Galleries*, based in Dallas, established in the early 1980s, is carving out specialties in coins, sports collectibles, and memorabilia. There are hundreds of fine quality regional auction companies across the United States.

The regional or specialized auction company will usually have lower lot minimums, and they may be better suited to handle a larger variety of items for you in one sale. Unlike the major houses, where auctions most often are devoted to one category, such as furniture or modern paintings, some smaller auction companies conduct **"estate auctions,"** at which different types of property will be sold, or property from different estates will be combined into one sale. It's more common at regionals to see furniture, paintings, jewelry, and carpets, all auctioned together. These companies may be better able to sell larger quantities of smaller valuable items such as books, glass, other decorative arts, or historical memorabilia, especially if it is of interest to the area.

Auction results at the regional level are often closely watched by experts and top collectors. Many regional companies have opened up their auctions recently to online bidding, so the audiences are wider.

You may choose a regional auction company, rather than one of the two majors, for fine and valuable items for a variety of reasons:

- they may be geographically convenient
- there may be an expert on the staff who is particularly knowledgeable about your items
- you may have items that sell better in your area, such as works by artists of local importance, historical pieces, or furniture from your region
- you may be able to get your items into a sale sooner
- certain of the costs such as catalog fees and shipping might be lower

You should feel free to consult with more than one auction company to decide which is the best showcase for your pieces. Ask them to provide you with results from previous auctions, their opinions on the current market conditions, who might be buying at their sales and what other factors may influence demand.

Regional auction companies have expertise with period antiques, fine art, historical memorabilia, decorative arts, rare books and manuscripts, nineteenth- and early-twentieth-century porcelain, china and art glass, carpets, and some types of collectibles and entertainment memorabilia. If you have done a good job with your inventory, you can discuss it with the auction company staff, possibly on the telephone, and they will give you an idea which of your items may be suitable for the type of sales they conduct.

## LOCALS AND LIQUIDATORS

All large cities and most small ones will have local auctioneers who can handle the sale of estates and household contents. Some of the small and local auction companies operate on two tiers:

- evaluate and process the sale of more valuable items, and
- conduct liquidations of less desirable or unwanted household goods.

The liquidator may actually auction the lower priced property or simply conduct an "estate buyout," offering you a cash settlement for the items that do not have much value. They will often haul away trash and clean up the house for you if you are moving. The buyout value may be very little, often just a few hundred dollars, but they provide a service in disposing of items you will probably have little success in selling.

If the auction company doesn't conduct buyouts or liquidations they will probably be able to give you a referral to someone who does this.

Local auction companies are suitable for:

- late-nineteenth- and early-twentieth-century antiques
- household items like china, glass, and silver, which may not have importance as antiques
- less valuable "vintage" furniture and reproduction antiques
- decorative paintings and other types of art, which may not be signed or identifiable
- family jewelry
- good quality reproduction rugs
- small antique items such as clocks, cameras, appliances, tools, kitchen utensils, music boxes, commemorative ware, and other accessories

You may decide to deal with a local auction company for more valuable items as well simply because of the convenience of a nearby location. Dealers shop at local auctions looking for bargains, and some bidding may get competitive.

## HOW TO WORK WITH AUCTION COMPANIES

All auction companies are open to calls from people who have items for sale. You can find auction companies:

- on their own websites,
- in your local yellow pages, or
- through a referral from an estate planning attorney or local antique or art dealer.

Many local and regional auction companies have **appraisal clinics**, where you can bring items in for a free evaluation. In addition to viewing photos from you by mail or email, they will respond to telephone inquiries and arrange appointments with you to see your items where possible.

## COMMISSIONS AND FEES

In most auction situations, you can expect the **seller's commission** to be between **15 and 25%**. The higher the price of the item, the lower the percentage will be. The auction staff will discuss **estimates** with you and what kind of **reserves** are appropriate. **Shipping costs** will be at your expense, so bear this in mind when considering a major auction in New York!

**Catalog fees** are charged by most auction companies; this is a kind of listing fee for having the item included in the catalog with a photograph. Catalog fees at major auction companies can be hefty—several hundred dollars per item is not uncommon—so be sure to ask about this before agreeing to consign your item for sale.

The auction company will tell you how long it will take to receive your proceeds; typically thirty days or so after the sale.

When dealing with local auctioneers, set up an appointment for them to evaluate your household contents, and be sure you get an explanation of exactly what kind of services they provide. Ask for references. All auction companies are regulated by the states in which they do business, should be licensed and bonded, and may be affiliated with state auction associations. *The National Auctioneers Association* has a referral service on their website, which you can use to access lists of member auction companies in your area.

Whether you are working with a top international auction firm or a local one, *don't be afraid to ask questions.* No matter how much knowledge the auction experts seem to have, remember that you are bringing them items to sell, and therefore contributing to their business. Make sure you understand all the details and read any contract you are given to sign.

## ESTATE SALES

An **estate sale** is usually conducted inside your home or the home of a person who has passed away where the contents are for sale. Buyers—many of them dealers, collectors, and hobbyists—come to the home to examine the items at close range.

You would not choose to have an estate sale if you only had a few items for sale; the nature of the sale implies that a large number of diverse household items are going to be featured.

There are two kinds of estate sales:

- A sale that is managed by a **professional estate sale organizer**, some-one who is in the business of conducting these sales regularly and has a following of customers who will attend your sale
- A sale you **conduct yourself** in the manner of a **yard or garage sale**— you do the advertising and attract your own customers

You can find an estate sale coordinator in the yellow pages or online. A better way to look for a reputable one is to ask for a referral from an estate planning attorney, a local realtor, appraiser, or antique dealer. Another easy way to find one is to watch the newspaper for notices of sales in your area. Go over and check it out. You can usually find the sale coordinator and perhaps get a minute to chat or at least get a business card.

## WHAT DOES THE ESTATE SALE PROFESSIONAL DO?

Basically, the estate sale professional comes in and runs the show. The work for you *should* be minimal.

The estate sale professional will:

- identify, value, and price your items or work together with you to do so
- promote and advertise the sale and draw buyers
- be on hand at the sale with staff persons to handle sales and payments
- clean things up when the sale is over and help you dispose of unsold property

If your home is for sale and you need to remove the contents before the close of escrow, the estate sale professional will work with your realtor on the best strategies for clearing the home of property so it can be shown to its best advantage.

In return for doing all this, the estate sale professional will take a **percentage of the proceeds** of the sale, usually somewhere between **30** and **35%**.

## CHECK OUT LOGISTICS

Before you decide an estate sale is right for you, consider the following:

If you live in a planned development, retirement community, condo, or co-op, check with your association to see if estate sales are permitted in your home. The estate sale professional may also know if your neighborhood requires any kind of permit before conducting a sale.

Do you have enough room, and the right kind of access to your home, to admit a good-sized crowd of people who will be wanting to move around and examine your items? Is there outdoor space such as a yard or driveway where some kinds of items can be safely displayed? Is there adequate parking available on your street or in the immediate vicinity?

In order for an estate sale to be successful, people need to be able to get to the sale and not have to wait an unreasonable amount of time for others to pass through the house. You can get quite a large early crowd if the estate sale professional does a good job of promoting the sale. One of the most unpleasant things about attending a sale is standing outside waiting to get in because the house will only accommodate a few shoppers at one time!

If your home is currently being occupied, you will want to sequester certain rooms and only permit access to areas where your merchandise will be displayed.

## PLANNING THE SALE

The estate sale coordinator should meet personally with you initially at no charge. Plan the meeting at the home where the sale will take place so the coordinator can inspect the premises, see the items you plan to sell, and advise you whether the sale is feasible.

Ask the estate sale professional how she or he plans to promote the event: does she or he have a mailing list? A website? Will there be signs in the neighborhood? Personally, I can never resist an estate sale if I happen to be driving by. The brighter and more professional-looking the sign, the better. Remember that one of the reasons you are hiring a professional is so they will bring buyers to your sale.

The estate sale coordinator will suggest the pricing of your items. She or he may possibly be an appraiser or have other credentials, such as experience as a dealer. The estate sale professional, like an appraiser, should *not* offer to buy any items from you or allow any of her staff to make offers to you. If you have questions about the valuations or want to have more input, discuss this when you're planning the sale. Remember, though, that the estate sale coordinator has experience selling items like yours. She has a feeling for what her customers will pay and what they like to buy.

## SHOP AROUND

Plan to interview at least two different companies so you can compare fees and services. Many estate sale professionals offer buyout liquidations of unwanted items (meaning the disposal of items not valuable enough to interest their customers). If they don't, they should refer you to someone who can remove the remaining items. Many estate sale organizers will pack unsold items for you and arrange for donations to charities (see chapter 18), obtaining the tax receipts on your behalf. Don't let someone conduct an estate sale and then leave you with the further task of cleaning up and disposing of unsold property.

Don't be afraid to ask questions or to ask for references. Make sure the estate sale company has a business license, and find out what kind of insurance coverage they have. Will they provide locked display cases for valuable items? What other security or safety issues should be discussed? If they provide you with a contract, make sure you understand the terms.

Make sure you get all your questions answered and feel comfortable with the situation before you make final arrangements for the sale. Estate sale professionals are usually "people oriented," and have experience putting on successful events.

## AT THE ESTATE SALE

Make sure your items are clean and attractively displayed. The best estate sales have a lot of pretty, clean, inviting, or interesting-looking items that draw attention. People like to handle and rummage through things at a sale. Try to have some stacks of books or racks of vintage clothing. Smaller items are easier for people to buy on impulse, although dealers often pull up to estate sales with trucks, planning to haul away furniture.

Most of the time at estate sales the items will be marked with tags or signs. I have been to a few sales where nothing is marked and you have to ask the price of everything, but honestly, I don't recommend this. If the sale is crowded and buyers always need to flag down a salesperson to negotiate a price, it slows things down. If buyers want to make an offer, for multiple purchases, for example, they usually will feel free to do so.

You will probably be advised *not* to spend the day of the estate sale on the premises. Opinions on this may vary, but you may find it harder than you expect to see familiar family possessions being handled by strangers and possibly to hear people muttering "they want $65 for *this*?" Don't, however, deal with any estate sale company that *prohibits* you from coming by on sale day. It's your merchandise and you should see what's going on if you choose.

Estate sales are an efficient way to attract multiple buyers and turn a houseful of items into cash. Make sure you are dealing with a qualified, reputable professional, don't worry about selling everything for "top dollar," and you will be pleased with the results.

## THE YARD-OR-GARAGE-TYPE ESTATE SALE

If you decide you don't need an estate sale coordinator to help you, you can conduct your sale on your own, just as you would have a yard sale. You might decide to do this if the advantages of working with a professional estate sale company—advertising, a following of clients, pricing and cleanup services—don't seem worth the percentages they charge.

A yard or garage sale can be advertised as an estate sale even if you are running it yourself. It can be a family project, and you *will* need volunteers, so get the kids or grandkids involved and have fun with it! Your "staff" will assist you in cleaning, organizing, and displaying the items, handling sales, answering questions, and keeping an eye on things.

Check out any local restrictions to having a yard sale in your community. Some cities have rules about where signs can be affixed or whether a permit is needed. Use as many *free* sources of advertising as you can find: supermarket or community center bulletin boards, free classifieds, your homeowner's association or town website. On the Thursday and Friday before the weekend of your sale, run the ad in your local newspaper.

Be sure to inform your neighbors you are planning to have a sale, and find out in advance about any parking problems or restrictions that could arise. Make sure your homeowner's policy is up-to-date—most policies will cover you in a liability or situation as long as you are not running a regular business on your property, but check with your insurance company to make sure.

## SALE TIPS—PRICING AND DISPLAYING YOUR ITEMS

When you conduct your own estate sale, you won't have professional help in identifying or establishing value for your items. You can do this yourself using guides, eBay sales, and some of the other resources we discussed in chapter 3. Remember that people are coming to your sale to find bargains, and that the purpose of having the sale is to sell things. If you have information or history about some of your items, make up a file card and write a few notes on it that will be of interest to the potential purchaser. Offer to include any original receipts or other documentation you may have that adds to the item's provenance. Other tips:

- Items on tables are easier to examine than on the ground or in boxes. You can consider renting tables from a party supply company, or building them of plywood. Mark items with price tags or signs—don't stick adhesive tags onto books or anything else on paper or any other surface that will be marred by adhesive residue.
- A hanging rack for clothing is nicer than piles or boxes. If you have appliances, clocks, power tools, automated toys, or watches, make a note on the price card stating if the item is in working order. Keep glass items near a grassy or carpeted area, so they are less likely to fall and crash on cement.
- Consider having a locked case for valuables, and/or keeping a table for more valuable items inside the house, where someone will be able to watch them more closely.
- Buy a pad of receipt forms at a drugstore or office supply chain in case someone requests one; carry your cash and change (have plenty of small bills) with you in a belly or fanny pack at the sale, it's safer than having a cash box, which you can't constantly keep an eye on.

Yard sales are fun but a bit of work. Don't be surprised if you feel exhausted when it's over! Make sure you allocate enough time to do it all, and get help from those family volunteers. Have a plan of what you're going to do with unsold items when the sale is over—are they being donated, stored, moved? If so, make sure you have boxes and a plan of action ready.

## WORKING WITH DEALERS

The local **antique shop, art gallery, jewelry store, or coin and stamp emporium** should still be counted as an important resource where you can get items evaluated and possibly find a buyer for your valuables. In the "old days," this was one of the only ways you could get a professional to help you identify or value a collectible item.

Now we have the internet, a boom in published price guides, more access to auction companies, as well as eBay. But the dealer's eye at close range is a very valuable tool, and sometimes the dealer's offer will be the quickest and most convenient way to sell an item.

Before you rush over to a local shop with something you want to identify, keep in mind that the dealer is in business to make money. He or she will expect to purchase or consign an item from you at substantially less than the price he will sell it for. Don't be surprised or insulted—this is normal. The dealer has the overhead of running his shop, utilities, insurance, often employees. The offer he presents may be as little as 20 or 30% of what the eventual selling price will be, or as much as 40 or 50%.

Most dealers prefer to **purchase outright**, but some will consider **consignments** (accepting the item from you for a period of time for sale, and then paying you a percentage of the proceeds if and when it sells). There are some antique stores that welcome consignments and work this way on a regular basis, and others that only buy. A reputable dealer should discuss all the options with you and be forthcoming about the realistic value of your articles. Knowledge about the identity and potential worth of your items will help you deal effectively with him.

There are many advantages to working with dealers, including **convenience**, and the certainty of an **immediate sale**, often for cash, instead of waiting weeks or months for an auction with no guarantee of the outcome. There are no shipping expenses for you, no worries about items being damaged in transit, and no waiting for your payment.

## WHEN SHOULD I SELL TO A DEALER?

Accepting a dealer's offer may be the best option for you if:

- you have an immediate need for liquidity
- you have a large collection of items of moderate value, many of which may not sell on their own
- you have items that need professional repair or restoration
- the dealer is a *specialist* in the exact type of item you have, for instance, he regularly represents the works of an artist, sells a specific kind of

book like military or medical titles; or works closely with clients looking for a certain style of furniture

- you have midrange items like jewelry or silver, which can be difficult to sell for high prices, or you don't want to risk breaking or damage by selling and shipping them yourself
- if you don't want to spend time on other methods of selling

## KNOWLEDGE IS POWER

What you have learned about possible values will enable you to make a well-informed decision about whether the dealer's offer to you is attractive.

You will find all kinds of dealers, just as there are all kinds of people. Some will only be interested in making a very large profit, and some will be more open to talking with you about the realistic price of an item and how much of that he or she can afford to pay you.

The more you understand about the role each of you plays in the transaction, the better the negotiations will go. If you can't come to an agreement or feel the price offered is too low for you to accept, just pass, and look for another way to sell your item. Most dealers will honor an offer they made for some time, so you can always go back later if you so decide.

## 16

# SELLING ON
# EBAY

EBay has created a revolution by providing a mass market for antiques, collectibles, and a host of other items previously only sold
in small stores, at antique shows or malls, or at more conventional auction
houses.

The volume and scope of eBay are increasing daily. Over a *hundred
million items* are listed every month, and not just in the collectibles area.
Real estate, new cars, electronics, and computer equipment also change
hands. The online "flea market" that began because one of its founders
collected Pez dispensers is now a modern institution operating in over
twenty countries, with over 150 million members. As CEO Meg Whitman sometimes points out, if eBay were a country in the world, it would
rank in the top ten in population—as measured by its over 100 million users
worldwide.

EBay is frequently changing, improving, and updating its site. If you
can't locate something mentioned in this chapter, it may have been moved
or updated. Go to the Site Map or access Live Help on the home page and
ask how to find it.

## GETTING TO KNOW EBAY

Before you decide if eBay is for you, you can spend some time learning your way around.

To start, go to the *eBay* **home page**. The main eBay areas can be accessed from the boxes to the right of the multicolored eBay logo. You can get acquainted by clicking on the "**Help**" box, and going to the **Learning Center** (under "related links" on the left side of the page). There you can take an audio tutorial about buying and selling.

You can also browse other topics in the Help area and learn about eBay's **policies, rules, fees, security, and community**. There's a **glossary** to get you familiar with some of the terms used on eBay, even a list of commonly used abbreviations in item descriptions.

Many guide books devoted to eBay are available. I have listed a few in the bibliography. You can find them at bookstores or pick up a new or used copy from an online dealer like Amazon.

Or click on "**eBay University**," on the Learning Center's page. Here, if you don't feel confident using eBay on your own, you can enroll in an **online course**, for around $20. EBay University also conducts live, in-person classroom sessions in many U.S. cities. You can find a location near you in the drop-down menu "Register Now" at the bottom of the page—just choose "find more locations" if you don't see your city listed.

## WHAT'S FOR SALE

Even without "formal education," you can learn a lot about what's selling on eBay by becoming a browser. You can learn what other people are selling, how they're identifying and describing their items, and what buyers are bidding on.

Click on the box that says "**Buy**," at the top of the main page, and you'll be taken to the millions of items for sale on eBay. You can use the search bar near the top of the page, just below where it says "Buy," to get an idea how certain items are listed.

On eBay all items for sale are sorted by **categories**. Some items are listed in multiple categories, or specific subcategories, for instance a manufacturer, period, or style.

Let's say you want to look for some examples of Depression Glass. Type "Depression Glass" in the search bar, and you'll be asked to select a category. If you choose "**all categories**" for your search criteria, you will be taken to a page that shows all the Depression Glass listings. You'll see that most of them are listed under the **Pottery and Glass heading**, under the **subcategory Depression**. There are also subcategories for different manufacturers. The subcategory headings on the left will tell you in parentheses how many listings there are in each.

## SEARCHING LISTINGS AND CATEGORIES

You can search items by **price**, from lowest or highest, or by the **time frame of the listing**, from "**ending soonest**" to "**newly listed**." There are also options for distance and payment method. To access any listing, just click on it. See how easy that was? You're already browsing listings.

Choosing the right category to list your items can be an important factor in attracting bidders. This is why it's important to study listings for awhile. Browse general categories such as Antiques and Collectibles to see how many sublistings there are and to get ideas where your items may fit. Try some general searches for items that are similar to yours.

For example, if you have some toy soldiers, but aren't sure if they fit the category of "toy soldiers" or "action figures," try the search on "Toy Soldiers," under "all categories."

How about a handwoven Mexican shawl? You'll find some listed in the Clothing, Shoes, and Accessories category, but also a few in the Collectibles category under "Ethnicities." Rock and roll tour T-shirts? Some are found under the "clothing" categories, but you might get better results listing in the music memorabilia category.

Items for sale on eBay can be listed in more than one category, but you will pay extra listing fees for this. It's best to familiarize yourself first with what is selling where. Buyers don't always search for a specific item. They browse, too, looking around for interesting merchandise, and many will shop in favorite categories or **use category-specific favorite searches**.

## THE EBAY COMMUNITY

You can browse many information resources on eBay without being a member. The **Community** box (one of the main areas in the boxes at the top of the main page) will take you to eBay's **discussion forum, message board, and chat area**.

Here you can read questions and answers on a huge variety of topics. Try the **"Answer Center"** for general inquiries about listings and selling. The **category-specific forums** often contain FAQs (frequently asked questions) and special help for new sellers. Antiques has an **"Official What Is It Thread"** where you can post photos of things you can't identify. Books has interesting info on book repairs, dating of bindings, reference guides, and library links.

You can read the questions and answers others have posted here, but can't reply or post a question yourself, or visit a chat room, until you're an eBay member.

In the Community area you can also find **collectors' clubs**, groups from various **regions** around the country, announcements, and bulletin boards, eBay Radio, Q&A chat rooms, **category-specific chat** for over twenty-five collectible categories, and a charitable site called Giving Works, where you can learn how to buy or sell an item to support a nonprofit cause.

In the Community area, take time to review the **Rules and Policies** of eBay before you start selling. There is a list of **prohibited items** (things like firearms, plants, tobacco, and alcohol); advice about how to deal with potential problems; information on privacy issues, identity protection, feedback, and policies on intellectual property rights; and general rules about buying and selling.

## NEXT STEP—REGISTER

When you feel you've gained a little experience getting around on eBay, you're ready to become a member. You will want to be able to track the results of items that are for sale, and you need to be an eBay member to access completed auction results. Becoming a member is free and doesn't obligate you to buy or sell anything.

Go ahead and click on the blue word, "register," above the main eBay area boxes at the top of the home page. You will be guided through the registration process, and there's live help available if you have a question. You will have to pick an **eBay user name** and supply a credit or debit card number just for identification and security purposes. You won't be billed anything, and you won't have to use that particular card to pay for eBay purchases or fees.

Once you're an eBay member, you can gain access to **auction results**, make purchases as a buyer, and set up a **Seller's Account** so you can list your items. As a seller, you will have to provide a bank account and/or credit card specifically for the purpose of paying your eBay fees. EBay provides an invoice once a month of all the activity charged to your account, and you can access your updated account on eBay at any time.

## HOW MUCH DOES IT COST?

There's no charge to purchase an item on eBay. Packing and shipping expenses for every item are paid by the buyer. These costs should be itemized by the seller on the listing page. When you are the winning bidder of an item, you will receive a Winning Bidder notification from eBay and usually an invoice for your item from the seller, including shipping charges.

Most buyers and sellers on eBay also register with *PayPal*, eBay's online payment processing system. You can register on PayPal using a bank account, credit card, or both, and use the account to pay for items you purchase as well as receive payments from buyers who purchase your items.

## PAYPAL FEES

PayPal is free to buyers. For sellers, there is a fee that starts at 3% for the smallest amounts and decreases for larger ones if you have a business account that accepts credit card payments. If you want to avoid these, you can have a personal account, which does not charge any fees, but buyers will not be able to make credit card purchases from you.

Because PayPal is convenient and widely used, it is preferred by most buyers and sellers, but you don't have to use it or accept it. Personal checks, cashier's checks, money orders, and some other online payment services such as BidPay are commonly used on eBay.

## EBAY SELLING FEES

There are two basic kinds of seller's fees on eBay, the **listing fees** and the **final value fee**. Listing fees start at around **35 cents per item**, and various features of a listing, such as photos, can cost more. When an item is sold, a small percentage of the selling price, usually averaging around 1%, is charged to your eBay account.

For a complete breakdown of Seller's fees, click on the Help box, then go to Selling. You'll find a detailed fee schedule under the heading "Selling Your Item." PayPal also has a fee schedule, which you can access from "Help" at the top of the PayPal home page. You don't have to register or sign in to either eBay or PayPal to read about the fees.

## SHIPPING AND PHOTOS

Two things you will have to learn to do when you sell on eBay are how to:

- estimate shipping costs
- take photos of your items with a digital camera

You will be responsible for packing and shipping the items that you sell. Most buyers will expect to receive their items promptly, especially if they pay quickly. You may receive a PayPal payment from a buyer within minutes of an auction's end, so be prepared to pack that item and get it in the mail to your customer swiftly! If you can't ship the item right away, an email to the buyer thanking them for their payment and telling them when they can expect delivery is part of good customer service.

Most sellers quote shipping costs in the terms section of their listings. You can also set up a calculator where the buyer can enter his zip code and find the shipping cost. If you are going to sell a lot of items on eBay, invest in a **postal scale** so you can weigh your items and packaging and provide accurate shipping rate quotes. You can order packing and shipping materials directly from eBay, including scales and postage meters, or find them at box and packing supply stores.

**PayPal Shipping** enables you to pay for postage and print postal labels directly from your PayPal account. To do this, you need to be familiar with the different postal services (Air Mail, Priority Mail, Parcel Post, and Media Mail are some of them). UPS and Federal Express can also be used, but can be more expensive than mail. Delivery confirmations and insurance are commonly included. EBay has a direct link to the **U.S. Postal Service** website, and you can also take a **Shipping Tutorial** in the Learning Center.

If you don't have a digital camera, visit your local electronics retailer and have a salesperson show you how to use one, or get help from that shutterbug in your family. It's surprisingly easy, and you don't have to be a camera buff. Experiment to find the best place around the house to take your photos. Sometimes natural light works best, against a neutral background. Study other sellers' listings or get help in the forums to improve your photography skills.

## CONDITION, CONDITION

When you start selling, I recommend starting off with lower-priced, but quality articles where you have seen comparable or similar sales in completed items. Some of the easiest mistakes to make involve under- or overestimating shipping costs, and not being specific enough about the condition of an item. Be conservative and don't overlook flaws; nothing is as disappointing to an eBay buyer as receiving an item that is not in the condition described in the listing. Many sellers don't offer a return policy, but doing so will give prospective buyers more confidence. Do what you can to provide the highest degree of customer service: this includes sending prompt invoices, notifying buyers when you have shipped their items, and giving positive feedback to buyers who pay promptly.

## SELLING WITH TRADING ASSISTANTS

The **Trading Assistants** program was begun by eBay in 2002 to help inexperienced sellers. The TA program also serves people who want access to eBay to sell their goods but don't have the time, the know-how, or the inclination to manage their listings by themselves.

Since it began, the Trading Assistant business has become an industry of its own, spawning several huge franchises and public companies. There are two kinds of Trading Assistants, or TA's as we'll call them:

- the **individual** who generally works at home
- the "**drop-off**" **center**, which operates like a store with regular business hours. Drop-off center chains include the Auction Farm, I-Sold-It-On-EBay, and many others.

## WHAT DOES A TA DO?

A TA will take your items, photograph them, list them under his or her own eBay username, pay all the listing and final value fees, collect the payment from the buyer, and handle the packing and shipping. In other words, you provide the item, the TA does all the work!

When your items have sold, the TA should provide you with an accounting, and will charge you a percentage of the gross sales, typically anywhere from 15 to 35%. You will receive payment from the TA for the value of your items minus the fees incurred and the TA's commission. TA's can charge anywhere from 20 to 35%, which is somewhere in the ballpark of regular auction and estate sale commissions.

The TA's experience and feedback rating will be a factor in attracting bidders to your items. You can monitor the auctions while your items are selling—it's a perfect way to experience eBay and learn how to sell.

Working with a TA is a little like having a "virtual estate sale." Some of them help you identify and value your items, and will research what similar items have been selling for on eBay. Some TA's might be experts or specialists in certain areas, like books or jewelry. Many of them will visit your home, much the way an estate sale professional would, to give you a no-obligation evaluation of your items and discuss the details of how your selling arrangement will work.

## HOW TO FIND A TA

Click on "Services" above the boxes on the eBay home page, and then look on the right side of the page under **Selling Services—Listing Solutions—Trading Assistants**. You can conduct a simple or advanced search for a TA in your geographical area or zip code. The TA listings should contain phone numbers and information about the TA's services, including their specialty areas. You can call or email the TA to ask questions, set up a meeting, or get feedback on some of your digital photos.

To qualify as a TA and be listed in the TA directory on eBay, a member must have a high positive feedback rating and a relative degree of selling experience. They also have to be a member in "good standing," which is a way of saying that they have to display business integrity. You can meet or speak with more than one TA to make sure you find someone you feel comfortable with.

EBay is the fastest growing company in history, and it is a phenomenon that is helping many people unleash their entrepreunerial spirit. Whether you sell a few pieces or become a Power Seller, work with a TA or on your own, you will be participating in an amazing phenomenon. Don't be afraid to try it!

## OTHER ONLINE SELLING RESOURCES

EBay may be the biggest, but not the only place online where you can list things for sale. **Bidville** bills itself as "the alternative auction site," and is considerably smaller than eBay. However, the smaller number of listings makes it easy to browse, and the site is user-friendly. Sports and historical memorabilia as well as all sorts of small collectibles are active on Bidville.

**Amazon** also has auctions, with books, sports memorabilia, and jewelry, as well as noncollectible categories such as electronics and photography equipment.

**Online Classified Ad Sites** are too numerous to list here. Some local newspapers and other publications such as *Recycler* have them, as well as national sites such as *U.S. Free Ads*, *Sell.Com*, and *Craig's List*.

Collectibles portals such as *Online Collectibles* and *Internet Collector's Bazaar* feature classified areas where individuals can list items for sale, or want ads, where collectors can post a message if they are looking for a special object.

Classifieds, both online and the old-fashioned print kind, are a good idea for used property that doesn't fall into the "collectible" category. There are other types of online services sprouting up every day, offering "virtual" yard sales, consignments, appraisals, pick-up and delivery, and other services.

## TRUST AND SAFETY

As always, if you contact any new business where your items or any personal information may be involved, be sure to:

- get references
- find out if they have any kind of business license and/or insurance
- understand the details of any agreement you make
- generally proceed with caution until you have good reason to believe it's a reputable concern

The auction and collectibles business is moving increasingly online, and there are many opportunities for ethical and entreprenurial folks to start creative businesses. However, be thorough and check things out. There are online safety groups such as *Wired Safety* and *Scambusters*, which offer tips on dealing with online businesses. *AuctionBytes*, an auction community site, has a list of fraud resources links and other advice for participating in online auctions.

# 17

# CHARITABLE DONATIONS

A nne was sitting in her doctor's waiting room, leafing through a magazine. Her doctor was behind schedule as usual! The doctor's wife, Julia, was an avid antique collector and decorator, and the coffee table in front of Anne was piled with many art, antique, and design magazines. Julia had decorated her husband's office tastefully with luxurious Oriental rugs, interesting prints, and folk art.

Anne's doctor was always eager to talk about Julia's latest acquisitions. Today, however, Anne was glancing at her watch. She had a lunch appointment and would be late if the doctor kept her waiting very much longer.

Suddenly her attention was captivated by a photo in the magazine she was reading. She saw something that looked very familiar.

Years ago, in the early 1960s, Anne and her husband David had purchased a new ranch-style home. Anne's preferred style of decorating was traditional, but David was more adventurous, preferring vibrant colors and modern designs. Anne agreed with David that the family room of their home could use an updated look. They went shopping for furniture and purchased two starkly modern chrome chairs with interesting fabric seats, an unusual chrome and plastic "shell" shaped chair, and a chrome and leather chaise. To go with the chairs they had bought some inexpensive modern lamps, Plexiglas tables, and a low-slung sofa.

Over the years the modern furniture began to seem dated to Anne, and David agreed. The room had a large stone fireplace, and they redecorated with a warmer, Southwestern theme. David took the chrome furniture into the basement and covered the chairs with sheets. The lamps and sofa went to Anne's daughter's New York apartment; posters and other odds and ends from the room had long since been donated to a local rummage sale. Anne thought from time to time about calling a local charity and having someone come and take the chairs away. But something always stopped her. They had been a fun and somewhat carefree purchase and brought back good memories. The chairs were still downstairs, their coverings collecting years of dust.

Anne stared at the magazine open in her lap. There was a full-page ad for an upcoming Sotheby's auction featuring "important twentieth-century design." In the photo was a chrome chair almost exactly like one of the chairs in Anne's basement!

Anne knew little about antiques, but she knew if something were to be auctioned at Sotheby's, it must have value.

"The doctor will see you now." A door to the inner office opened and a nurse startled Anne out of her absorption. She took the magazine with her into the doctor's examining room. When he came in, he was surprised to find Anne poring over the photo.

"Look at this—these chairs are going to be in a Sotheby's auction. I have a pair very much like this one. I had no idea this kind of furniture was valuable."

"Do you know where they came from? Did you buy them?"

"Yes, David and I got them at the Knoll showroom, when it first opened, before they moved to the Design Center. David wanted to go contemporary, but we just did one room."

Anne's doctor looked at the picture and chuckled.

"Julia has been talking about how the prices of this stuff have skyrocketed. Maybe you should have them appraised. I'm sure Julia could refer you to someone."

"Appraised!" Anne was astounded by the idea of her nearly cast-off chairs having any value. "May I keep this magazine? I want to show it to David."

Anne brought the magazine home and that evening, she and David went down to the basement to look at the chairs under the sheets. One of them was indeed very similar to the piece in the Sotheby's ad.

"How do we know they aren't just reproductions?" Anne wondered.

"Why don't you ask Julia about it?" David suggested.

Julia was delighted to hear from Anne.

"I know just the person for you to call. I have a friend named James who is curator of the University's decorative arts museum," she told Anne. "In fact, they have been looking for pieces to add to their collection. Unless, of course, you want to sell them."

"A museum?" Anne had never heard of such a thing. She recalled David had been complaining at tax time. "Would we get a deduction?"

"Why don't you meet with James, and he can explain it all to you." Julia recited the phone number.

Anne and David still could not quite believe their vintage chairs would be of any interest to a museum. But when James arrived, he examined the chairs with a good deal of excitement.

"This recliner is definitely Marcel Breuer, a very early piece. The shell chair is Charles or Ray Eames, or maybe both. This pair could be Nelson or Harold Bartos. We have many of the early catalogs, and our archivist will research them. They're all excellent examples of the modern style. We would love to feature them in our upcoming exhibit, on loan from you of course."

Anne and David were thrilled that they were unexpectedly in the possession of potential museum pieces.

"Shouldn't we auction them at Sotheby's? Or keep them as an investment?"

"It seems to me they already were a pretty good investment," David replied. "We could take the money and invest in some of those paintings you've been wanting. We could use a tax write-off." He looked questioningly at James.

"As a museum we don't get involved in valuations, but we can refer you to a third party who will be qualified to appraise them," James told him.

"Then, if you are thinking of making a gift, you need to consult with your accountant, who can help you determine the exact value of the deduction. I do know that to receive the best benefit, the item you donate must be directly related to the mission and purpose of the organization. Because we are a decorative arts museum, promoting interest in this kind of item, these pieces would be qualified."

Anne and David eventually decided to make a gift of their chairs to the museum. An appraisal was performed, and reviewed by their accountant. Several months later they were thrilled to receive a catalog and an invitation to the opening of the exhibit in which their chairs were featured. The catalog listed the chairs as being from Anne and David's "collection."

"Too bad we really don't have a big collection," said Anne.

"You wanted to throw them away!"

"But I didn't. You know, David, I've been thinking about this room. . . . Maybe we should redecorate!"

"You know, I still like Modern. . . . " They both laughed.


## WHY DONATE?

Whether or not you have an unexpected museum piece like Anne and David's chairs, or you just have some boxes of things you don't want, you should know some of the general rules about **donating tangible personal property such as art and collectibles to charities**.

You may decide to donate for one of several different reasons:

- as a substitute for giving a gift of cash
- because you have something of value that is not something you like or want to keep
- you have duplicate items or many similar items
- the cost of selling an item—insurance, transport, storage—can reduce the potential sale price to a considerable extent, making a donation more financially advantageous than a sale
- you have some things that are not particularly salable, or in collectible condition, but would be usable by a charity

## WHAT IS THE TAX TREATMENT OF A PERSONAL PROPERTY DONATION?

There are two aspects to donating personal property:

- how is the **value** of the donated item determined?
- how much of a **deduction** are you able to take once the value has been established?

Charitable donations may be valued in two ways: the **fair market value** of the item, or the **cost basis**—the amount you paid when you acquired an item.

Donations of personal property work a little differently than donations of cash or stocks.

When you donate stocks to charity, the IRS permits a deduction which is always based on the fair market value. The price of the shares on the day you make the donation is the value. This is a good strategy to use with stocks that have appreciated, and not so useful with stocks that may have declined.

With tangible property like art, antiques, and collectibles, the IRS rules are more complex. Under *some circumstances* you are able to receive a fair market value deduction, but there may be other factors that will limit the deduction to your original cost, or "cost basis," in an item.

**IRS Publication 561** is called "Determining the Value of Donated Property." You can get this publication on the IRS website. Don't worry—it is surprisingly readable and understandable!

The IRS defines "Fair Market Value" as the price a piece of property would sell for on an open market, between a knowledgeable and willing buyer and seller.

In order for an item to qualify for Fair Market Value **(FMV)** as a donation, the following conditions must *generally* be met:

- The property must meet the **related use rule**. James referred to this in his conversation with Anne and David. It means that the institution to which the property is being donated must have a *mission or purpose that is directly related* to the type of item you are giving them.

- The gift must be made to a **public charity**. A family foundation, for example is considered a *private*, not a public charity. A donation of personal property to a private charity will generally need to be valued at cost basis, not FMV.
- The property must be **appraised** by a qualified professional, or other evidence of value is expected to be provided.
- The property must have **capital gain status**. **This means**: a sale at FMV on the date of the contribution would have resulted in a long-term gain. Under the current tax laws, the property needs to have been held by its owner for one year or more. Property inherited in an estate situation will generally carry long-term status assuming it had been held by the decedent **longer than a year**.
- Property held less than a year is said to have **ordinary income status**, similar to the way a short-term gain is taxed. The value for ordinary income property in a donation is **the *lesser* of the cost basis or the FMV**. If you purchased an item which has declined in value, the FMV is less than the cost basis, then you would be generally restricted to a FMV deduction.
- There are other situations where ordinary income status, or the lesser of cost basis or FMV, is the rule. These include: donations to charity auctions; items used in a trade or business, such as art donated by a professional dealer; copyrighted material; and certain other situations where the donor is aware of the intention to sell the donated property immediately for cash.

Let's look at some examples of the conditions we just discussed:

Sally donates a rare book collection to a library. She has owned the books longer than one year. This donation meets both the related use and capital gain rules, so she is entitled to value the collection at FMV for the donation.

Stephen donates a painting to a museum. He bought the painting for $10,000 less than a year ago, but the artist has since had a major exhibition, and an appraiser values the painting today at $20,000. The donation *meets the related use rule*, but Stephen must use $10,000 as the value. The painting does not have capital gain status—he has owned it less than one year.

Betsy wants to give a donation to an environmental charity she supports. But she is low on cash and asks the charity if she can give them some pieces of sculpture she has. The charity will sell the art and use the money to further its purposes. Betsy bought the sculptures in a gallery several years ago. The artist has become more famous, and the sculptures have since appreciated in value. But because the donation *does not meet the related use rule*, Betsy must use her *cost basis* as the value for the donation.

Jenny donates some of her vintage designer gowns to a charity auction, where they will be sold and the proceeds used to support breast cancer research. The FMV of the dresses today is less than what she originally paid. The property does not meet the related use rule, and additionally the donation will be sold at the auction to raise cash. In this example, Jenny must use **the (lower) fair market value** of the dresses as the value of the donation.

The IRS has a few other special rules for cars, boats, and other vehicles; scientific research equipment; and testamentary bequests.

## DONATIONS AND DEDUCTIONS

Once the value of the item to be donated has been established, the next step is to figure how much of that value is actually deductible on your tax return.

Under 2005 law, contributions of personal property are generally *deductible in the contribution year* up to an amount equal to 30% of the donor's **adjusted gross income (AGI)**, with a five-year carry forward of the unused portion.

This means if you want to donate a $100,000 painting, but your AGI is $200,000, you could use only $60,000 of the deduction (30% of $200,000) in the year it is donated, and carry forward the remaining $40,000.

Donations to nonpublic charities (such as family foundations) may result in a reduced eligible percentage of AGI.

## DON'T FORGET THE FORMS

For any charitable donation that exceeds $500, you will need to submit IRS **Form 8283, Noncash Charitable Contributions**, which will require you to list specifics such as cost basis, FMVs, and methods used to determine FMVs.

If a donation exceeds $5000, **you must get an appraisal**. Part B of the form, the **Appraisal Summary,** must be **filled in and signed and dated by the appraiser**.

For donations valued at $20,000 and more, a **complete copy of the appraisal** must accompany the tax form.

Most large donations, especially of art, are reviewed by the IRS's Art Panel.

## MORE STRATEGIES

There are more complex tax strategies available that can be used with personal property. Some of these include:

- donating property to a **Donor-Advised Fund, Charitable Remainder Trust, Charitable Lead Trust, or Charitable Gift Annuity;**
- **charitable "bargain sales"**—in which an item is sold to a charity for less than its FMV, providing some cash flow to the donor and a profit for the charity; and
- **fractional giving**—increasingly popular now that fine art values have been soaring well beyond the limits of the annual AGI limitations we discussed above. Fractional gifts are something like a gradual donation, or can be similar to giving a museum the right to hold and display the work for a portion of the year. Eventually the donation can be made permanent.

## INVOLVE THE CHARITY OR MUSEUM

The institution to whom you plan to donate property needs to be directly involved in receiving your gift, as well. Many people make bequests in wills, leaving items to museums, foundations, universities, and favorite charities, without knowledge of whether or not the lucky recipient organization will really want the gift.

Many museums, especially major ones, have detailed and long-range acquisition programs and may only be interested in very specific types of art. They may wish to have the right to sell a valuable piece you may give them and invest the proceeds in areas of greater interest to them. Some donors want to stipulate that their gift be displayed, which isn't always possible.

For substantial art gifts, **professional consultants** are sometimes employed to help a donor "place" a donation that will be accepted by the right museum.

Stephanie's father, Carl, left his extensive collection of history and law books to the library at his alma mater.

As executor of her father's estate, Stephanie was surprised to find that the university wanted to review the collection before accepting them, and also expected the estate to incur packing and shipping expenses.

"I thought they would be thrilled to have my father's library," Stephanie said. "I pictured a section in the library where they would be displayed, a plaque with my father's name. It was disappointing to feel I needed to convince them to accept the gift. If it were possible, I would have looked for another institution that would want the books, or I would have made a different kind of donation in my father's memory, a scholarship fund or a reading program."

Stephanie's experience was not unusual; in fact, many university libraries lately are asking to review lists of potential gifts of books, or are turning away donations altogether. However, countless other charities welcome book donations—the **American Medical Student Association** is one that welcomes used medical textbooks. There are many organizations that send books overseas to reading programs in developing countries.

## TALK TO THE PLANNED GIVING DEPARTMENT

Most universities, museums, and other major nonprofit institutions have **planned giving departments**. You can contact a representative and consult with them about future bequests as part of the estate planning process. Remember that donations have to fit the needs and plans of the institution. It's better to discuss it with them ahead of time and, if necessary, look for an organization that agrees to accept what you have to offer.

## DONATIONS ARE NOT ONLY FOR TAX DEDUCTIONS

After the death of her brother Greg, Julie donated several pieces of his art collection to the hospital where Greg had spent many weeks battling the final stages of a long illness.

"The financial aspects of the donation were unimportant to me," she explained. "My accountant explained about looking into a tax deduction, but I thought more about giving people at the hospital something to enjoy and distract them. The hospital was very pleased about it and agreed that it would be permanently on their walls, with a card beneath each piece acknowledging Greg. It gave me some comfort to know that other people might see and appreciate something that had been of value to him."

Charitable organizations need everyday items for use in shelters, rehab facilities, community centers, and other facilities. Other institutions are interested in any kind of item they can use to raise cash. Ordinary household property from estates can be used and is welcomed by a large variety of charities, many of whom will come and pick it up from you as a convenience.

## FIND OUT ABOUT DONATIONS

Local **grantmaking organizations** and **philanthropic advisors** can give advice to potential donors about how to find a charity that is a good "fit" for a donation you might have in mind, or help strategize a gifting program for you. Websites such as the *American Institute of Philanthrophy* and *Charity Navigator* help donors make informed decisions by providing financial information and ratings on charities, including how much of contributions is spent on expenses.

## TALK TO YOUR TAX AND LEGAL ADVISORS

Your **tax advisor, attorney, Certified Financial Planner (CFP), or all three** should assist you in making decisions about charitable donations. You can get a referral to a CFP from the *CFP Board of Standards*. If your accountant is not knowledgeable about the tax aspects of personal property donations, check with your state's **professional CPA organization** for a referral.

# EPILOGUE: FINDING THE TREASURES

What will be the collectibles of the future? Vintage cell phones, transistor radios, and early computers are already gaining in popularity. So are 1950s kitchen appliances, 1960s cocktail shakers, 1970s synthetic fabric swatches, and defunct stock certificates from 1990s dot-com companies. If history is any guide, the rare antique of the next century might be any commonplace item in the room where you're sitting now.

Most families will go through transitions, and experience letting go, not just of material possessions. Discovering value and sharing memories of favorite heirlooms is no subtitute for the loss of a loved one. But our connections to them can be made stronger through appreciation of favorite things they may leave to us.

Many people, like some of those in this book, find new hobbies, passions, and directions in collectibles. Antique and art lovers know there is much more than monetary value to a treasured object—there is also history, beauty, and something of the soul of the person who created the work.

Whether you decide to sell some of your valuables, give them away, or keep them in the family, learning more about them can be an adventure. And whether your family treasures turn out to be priceless rarities, or just everyday things that were lived with and loved, your knowledge and appreciation of them can be a valuable asset all its own.

# SUGGESTIONS FOR RESEARCH AND FURTHER READING

## ANTIQUES AND COLLECTIBLES—GENERAL

*Antique Trader Antiques and Collectibles Price Guide 2006.*

Chervenka, Mark. *Guide to Fake and Forged Marks.* Krause Publications, July 2002.

———. *Guide to Fakes and Reproductions.* Krause Publications, 2003.

Durdik, et al., eds. *Pictorial Encyclopedia of Antiques.* Hamlin, 1968. Out of print.

Kovel, Ralph, and Terry Kovel. *Kovels' Antiques and Collectibles Price List 2005.* Random House, 2005.

———. *Kovels' "Know Your Collectibles."* Random House, 1981.

Miller, Judith. *Collectibles Price Guide 2005.* DK Publishing, 2004.

Prisant, Carol. *Antiques Roadshow Collectible: The Complete Guide.* Workman Publishing, 2003.

Rosson, Joe L., and Helaine Fendelman. *Price It Yourself.* HarperCollins, 2003.

———. *Treasures in Your Attic.* HarperCollins, 2001.


## ART

Finch, Christopher, and Linda Rosenkrantz. *Sotheby's Guide to Animation Art.* Henry Holt, 1998.

Frank, Jeanne. *Discovering Art: A User's Guide to the World of Collecting.* Thunder's Mouth Press, 1997.

Hislop, Duncan. *Hislop's Official International Price Guide to Fine Art.* House of Collectibles, 2002.


## BOOKS

Ahearn, Allan, and Patricia Ahearn. *Collected Books: The Guide to Values 2002.* Putnam, 2001.

Tedford, Marie, and Pat Goudey. *The Official Price Guide to Collecting Books.* 5th ed. House of Collectibles, 2005.

Zempel, Edward N., ed. *First Editions: A Guide to Identification.* Spoon River Press, 2001.


## CERAMICS AND GLASS

Boggess, Bill. *American Brilliant Cut Glass.* Crown, 1977.

Edwards, Bill, and Mike Carwile. *Standard Encyclopedia of Carnival Glass.* Collector Books, 2002.

Husfloen, Kyle, and Pat McPherson, eds. *Antique Trader Pottery and Porcelain Ceramics Price Guide.* Krause Publications, 2003.

Lehner, Lois. *Lehner's Encyclopedia of U.S. Marks on Pottery, Porcelain, and Clay.* Collector Books, 1998.

Schroy, Ellen T. *Warman's Depression Glass Field Guide.* 2nd ed. KP Books, 2005.

Shuman, John A., III. *Art Glass: Identification and Price Guide.* Krause Publications, 2003.

## CHARITABLE GIVING

Kennedy, Michael B., et al. *Price-Waterhouse Cooper's Guide to Charitable Giving.* Wiley, 2002.

## COMICS

Overstreet, Robert M. *The Official Overstreet Comic Book Price Guide.* 36th ed. House of Collectibles, 2006.

Thompson, Maggie, et al. *2005 Comic Book Checklist and Price Guide: Comics Buyers Guide.* Krause Publications, 2004.

## EBAY

Gralla, Preston. *Teach Yourself eBay in a Snap.* Sams Publishing, 2004.

Griffith, Jim. *Official eBay Bible.* Gotham, 2003.

Miller, Michael. *Absolute Beginner's Guide to eBay.* 2nd ed. Que, 2004.

Wiggins, Pamela. *Buying and Selling Antiques and Collectibles on eBay.* Muska & Lippman, 2004.

## ESTATE PLANNING

Fleming, Edmund. *Estate Planning and Administration.* 2nd ed. Allsworth Press, 2004.

Palermo, Michael T. *AARP Crash Course in Estate Planning.* Sterling, 2004.

Platt, Harvey J. *Your Living Trust and Estate Plan.* Allsworth Press, 1999.

## FASHION

Eden, Diana, and Gloria Lintermans. *Retro Chic: A Guide to Fabulous Vintage and Designer Resale Shopping in North American and Online.* Really Great Books, 2002.

Harris, Kristina. *Collectors Guide to Vintage Fashions Identifications and Values.* Collector Books, 1998.

Lindroth, Linda, and Deborah Newell Tornello. *Virtual Vintage: The Insider's Guide to Buying and Selling Fashion Online.* Random House Trade Paperbacks, 2002.

Smith, Desire. *Vintage Style, 1920–1960*. Schiffer, 1997.

Turudich, Daniele. *The Vintage Fashion Directory: The National Source Book of Vintage Fashion Retailers*. Streamline Press, 2002.

## FURNITURE

Andrews, John. *Antique Furniture: Starting to Collect Guide*. Antique Collectors' Club, 1997.

Keno, Leigh, and Leslie Keno. *Hidden Treasures: Searching for Masterpieces of American Furniture*. Warner Books, 2000.

Lindquist, David P., and Caroline C Warren. *The Big Book of Antique Furniture*. Krause Publications, 2003.

Moran, Mark. *Antique Trader Furniture Price Guide*. Antique Trader Books, 2001.

Taylor, V. J. *Warman's How to Be a Furniture Detective*. Krause Publications, 2004.

Krause Publications, ed. *Furniture Field Guide: Values and Identification*. Krause Publications, 2002.

## JEWELRY

Bell, C. Jeanenne. *How to Be a Jewelry Detective*. A.D. Publishing, 2002.

———. *Answers to Questions about Old Jewelry*. 6th ed. Krause Publications, 2003.

Brunner, Gisbert L., and Christian Pfeiffer-Belli. *Wristwatches: A Handbook and Price Guide*. Rev. 4th ed. Schiffer Publishing, 2004.

Jordan, Roy. *Do It Yourself Guide to Jewelry Identification*. Jordan Enterprises, 1990.

Korda, Michael. *Marking Time*. Barnes & Noble, 2004.

Leshner, Leigh. *Vintage Jewelry: Price and Identification Guide, 1920 to 1940s*. Krause Publications, 2002.

———. *Warman's Jewelry Field Guide: Values and Identification*. KP Books, 2005.

Miller, Harice Simmons. *The Official Price Guide to Costume Jewelry*. House of Collectibles, 2002.

Pittman, Ann Mitchell. *Inside the Jewelry Box: A Collector's Guide to Costume Jewelry, Identification, and Values*. Collector Books, 2004.

Schumann, Walter. *Gemstones of the World*. Sterling, 1979.

Shugart, Cooksey, Tom Engle, and Richard Gilbert. *Complete Price Guide to Watches*. Collector Books, 2005.

## MEMORABILIA

Davis, William C., and Tria Giovan. *Memorabilia of the Civil War*. BDD Promotional Books, 1992.

Delph, John. *Firearms and Tackle Memorabilia: A Collector's Guide*. Schiffer Publishing, 1991.

Graf, John F. *Warman's Civil War Collectibles*. Krause Publications, 2003.

Heide, Robert, and John Gilman. *Disneyana: Classic Collectibles, 1928–1958*. Welcome Enterprises, 1994.

Schaeffer, Randy, and Bill Bateman. *Coca-Cola: The Collector's Guide to New and Vintage Coca-Cola Memorabilia*. Running Press Books, 1995.

Schroy, Ellen T. *Warman's Flea Market Price Guide*. 3rd ed. Krause Publications, 2003.

Summers, B. J., and Wayne Priddy. *Value Guide to Gas Station Memorabilia*. Collector Books, 1995.

Summers, B. J., and Bobby Summers. *Value Guide to Advertising Memorabilia*. Collector Books, 1998.

## MODERNISM

Fiell, Charlotte, and Peter Fiell. *Modern Furniture Classics: Postwar to Postmodern*. Thames & Hudson, 2001.

Greenberg, Cara. *Mid-Century Modern: Furniture of the 1950s*. Random House, 1995.

Habegger, Jerryll, and Joseph H. Osman. *Sourcebook of Modern Furniture*. 3rd ed. Norton, 2005.

Rago, David, and John Sollo. *Collecting Modern: A Guide to Midcentury Studio Furniture and Ceramics*. Gibbs-Smith, 2001.

## ORIENTAL RUGS

Eiland, Murray L. *Oriental Carpets: A Complete Guide, The Classic Reference*. Bulfinch, 1998.

## POSTCARDS

Mashburn, J. L. *Postcard Price Guide*. Colonial House, 2001.


## PRECIOUS METALS AND RARE COINS

Coin World, eds. *Coin World 2006 Guide to U.S. Coins: Prices and Value Trends*. Signet Books, 2006.

Guth, Ron. *Coin Collecting for Dummies*. Wiley, 2001.

Halperin, James L., et al. *The Collector's Handbook*. Ivy Press, 2000.

Travers, Scott A. *One Minute Coin Expert*. 5th ed. Random House Reference, 2004.

Yeoman, R. S., and Kenneth Bressett. *Official Price Guides to Coins: Blue Book and Red Book*. Whitman, 2005.


## SILVER

Dolan, Maryanne. *American Sterling Silver Flatware: 1830s–1990s, A Collector's Identification and Value Guide*. Krause Publications, 1992.

Ensko, Stephen G. C. *American Silversmiths and Their Marks*. Dover, 1983.

Fennimore, Donald, and Elizabeth Van Habsburg, eds. *Antique Hunter's Guide to American Silver and Pewter*. Black Dog & Leventhal, 2000.


## STAMPS

Chernoff, Ronni. *The World Encyclopedia of Stamps and Stamp Collecting*. Lorenz Books, 2005.

H. E. Harris & Co. *How to Collect Stamps*. Whitman Publishing, 2003.

MacDonald, David. *2005 Brookman Stamp Price Guide*. Brookman, Barrett & Worthen, 2004.

Sine, Richard L. *Stamp Collecting for Dummies*. Hungry Minds, 2001.


## TOYS AND DOLLS

Van Patten, Denise. *The Official Price Guide to Dolls*. House of Collectibles, 2005.

Pauline Cockrill, et al. *Teddy Bear Encyclopedia*. DK Publishing, 2001.

Marsh, Hugo. *Miller's Toys and Games: Antiques Checklist*. Mitchell Beasley, 1995.

O'Brien, Karen E., ed. *O'Brien's Toys*. 11th ed. Krause Publications, 2004.

Huxton, Sharon, and Bob Huxton. *Schroder's Collectible Toys: Antique to Modern Price Guide*. Collector Books, 2003.

Santelmo, Vincent. *The Complete Encyclopedia to GI Joe*. Krause Publications, 2001.

Johnson, Kent L., and Roger Carp, eds. *Greenberg's Guide Lionel Trains 2005 Pocket Guide*. Kalmback Publishing Company, 2004.

Melillo, Marcie. *The Ultimate Barbie Doll Book: Identification and Price Guide*. Krause Publications, 2004.

Johnson, Dana. *Toy Car Collectors Guide: Identification and Values for Diecast, White Metal, Other Automotive Toys, and Models*. Collector Books, 2002.

Sieber, Mary, ed. *Warman's Toys Field Guide*. Krause Publications, 2004.

Wells, Stuart W., III. *Warman's Star Wars Field Guide*. Krause Publications, 2005.

Stearns, Dan, ed. *Standard Catalog of Die-Cast Vehicles: Identification and Value*. Krause Publications, 2002.

Leffingwell, Randy. *Hot Wheels: 35 Years of Speed, Power, Performance, and Attitude*. Motorbooks International, 2003.

# INTERNET
# RESOURCE GUIDE

B elow are links to most of the sites I have referenced. Some of the sites are those of commercial dealers, and are listed because they provide background materials and information of interest.

## ANIMATION ART

*Animation Art Gallery*
 www.animationartgallery.com
 dealer in production art, articles, FAQs, glossary

*Van Eaton Galleries*
 www.vegalleries.com
 dealers in production art and modern animation collectibles

*Vintage Ink and Paint*
 www.vintageip.com
 dealers, appraisals, eBay auctions, restoration services, links

## ANTIQUES AND COLLECTIBLES—GENERAL

*About.Com*
>www.antiques.about.com
>articles, resources, tips, links, research

*ACDA, Antique and Collectible Association*
>www.antiqueandcollectible.com

*Antiques Roadshow Online*
>www.pbs.org/roadshow
>the website for the PBS series

*Antique Web*
>www.antiqueweb.com
>online magazine with articles and dealer directory

*BBC*
>www.BBC.co.uk/antiques/
>news, auctions and fairs guide, articles, information

*CBEL Search Page for Collecting*
>www.cbel.com/collecting/
>go from there

*Curioscape*
>www.curioscape.com
>links to dealers in every category of antique and collectible, classifieds

*Kovel's Online Guide*
>www.kovels.com
>detailed site from the authors of many price guides, including resources, databases, and Yellow Pages

*National Art and Antique Dealer Association of America*
>www.naadaa.org
>trade association of dealers; find a dealer by area of specialization

*National Association of Collectors*
>www.collectors.org
>collecting clubs, reference libraries

*World Collectors Net*
> www.worldcollectors.net
> collectibles portal with message boards, links, articles, web hosting, collecting search, and online magazine

## ANTIQUITIES

*Authentic Artifact Collector Association*
> www.theaaca.com
> Native American antiquities

*International Association of Dealers in Ancient Art*
> www.iadaa.org
> network of antiquities dealers

## APPRAISALS

*American Society of Appraisers*
> www.appraisers.org
> referrals and general info about appraisals

*Association of Online Appraisers*
> www.aoaonline.org

*International Society of Appraisers*
> www.isaappraisers.org

## ART

*Artfact*
> www.artfact.com
> fine art and antique auction previews, free and subscription services to research prices, catalogs, style guides, artist directory

*ArtNet*
> www.artnet.com
> free news of upcoming auctions, subscription service for results

*ArtPrice*

www.artprice.com

reference data bank on the art market and over 300,000 artists

*AskArt*

www.askart.com

American artist resource site with over forty thousand artists, glossary, art marketplace

## AUCTION COMPANIES

*Antiquorum*

www.antiquorum.com

specializing in watches and timepieces

*Bertoia*

www.bertoia.com

antique toys and collectibles

*Christie's*

www.christies.com

*Diamond International Galleries*

www.diamondgalleries.com

toys, comics, publishes the *Scoop*, a newsletter with news and prices

*Doyle's*

www.doylenewyork.com

antiques, jewelry, art, decorative arts

*Guernsey's*

www.guernseys.com

celebrity items, the unique and unusual

*Hake's*

www.hakes.com

Americana, political memorabilia, sports memorabilia, comics

*Heritage*

www.heritagegalleries.com

coins, celebrity memorabilia, historical memorabilia, art

*Hunt*

www.huntauctions.com

specializing in sports memorabilia

*Rago Arts*

www.ragoarts.com

specializing in Arts and Crafts furniture, ceramics, decorative arts

*RR Enterprises*

www.rrauction.com

celebrity and historical memorabilia

*Skinner's*

www.skinnerinc.com

Boston-based regional auction company

*Sotheby's*

www.sothebys.com

*Stack's*

www.stacks.com

rare coin specialists

*Swann's*

www.swanngalleries.com

books, maps, photographs, posters, prints, and drawings

*Theriault's*

www.theriaults.com

doll specialists, auctions, identifications, and appraisals

## BOOKS

*Advanced Book Exchange*

www.abebooks.com

inventories of over ten thousand book dealers

*Americana Exchange*

www.americanaexchange.com

rare book auction results and bibliographical database

*American Library Association Rare Book Section*
    www.rbms.nd.edu

*Antiquarian Booksellers Association of America*
    www.abaa.org
    links to research resources, questions and answers about book evaluation
    and repair, referrals to dealers

*Faded Giant*
    www.fadedgiant.com
    autographs, book values, other collecting resources

*International League of Antiquarian Booksellers*
    www.ilab-lila.com
    collecting resources and database

*SearchBiblio*
    www.searchbiblio.com
    18 million used, rare, out of print titles

## CERAMICS AND GLASS

*Best Pottery Info*
    www.best-pottery.info
    pottery markings, links, pottery information, and portal

*Bradshaw & Whelan Reference Books*
    www.ceramicbooks.com

*Ceramics Today Magazine*
    www.ceramicstoday.com

*Corning Glass Museum*
    www.cmog.org

*Glass Encyclopedia*
    www.glassencyclopedia.com

*International Ceramic Directory*
    www.ceramic-link.de
    international site with links to marks identification sites, books, muse-
    ums, galleries, magazines, and historical resources

## CHARITABLE GIVING

*American Institute of Philanthropy*
    www.charitywatch.org

*BBB Wise Giving*
    www.give.org

*Charity Navigator*
    www.charitynavigator.org

## CLASSIFIED ADS ONLINE

*Craig's List*
    www.craigslist.com

*Internet Collectors Bazaar*
    www.icollectorbazaar.com

*Recycler*
    www.recycler.net

*Sell.Com*
    www.sell.com

*US Free Ads*
    www.usfreeads.com

## COINS

*American Numismatic Association*
    www.money.org
    collecting and education about coins and paper money

*American Numismatic Society*
www.amnumsoc.com
fosters study and appreciation of coins and medals, library, informational resources, links

*Coin Facts*
www.coinfacts.com
extensive online coin encyclopedia

*Coin Resource*
www.coinresource.com
coin store, prices, articles, links to magazines

*Coin World*
www.coinworld.com
website of one of the leading coin magazines with news, classified ads, resources for new collectors, links to dealers, subscription coin values

*NGC, Numismatic Guaranty Company*
www.ngccoin.com

*PCGS, Professional Coin Grading Service*
www.pcgs.com
one of the foremost coin grading services with price guide, research archive, news, links, collectors club

*Superior Galleries*
www.superiorsc.com
auctions, appraisals, buy and sell

## COLLECTIBLES

*Internet Collector's Bazaar*
www.icollectorbazaar.com

*Online Collectibles*
www.onlinecollectibles.com

*The Online Collector*
www.theonlinecollector.com
links to a variety of dealers and collector sites

## COMICS

*CGC Comics Guaranty LLC*
   www.cgccomics.com
   comics grading

*Diamond Galleries*
   www.diamondgalleries.com
   sales, gallery, auctions, reference, newsletter

*Gemstone Publishing*
   www.gemstonepub.com
   publishers of the official *Overstreet Guide*

## DOLLS

*1853 Dollhouse*
   www.1853dollhouse.com
   antique dolls

*Anything Goes, Inc.*
   www.anythinggoesinc.net
   doll and teddy bear info

*Doll Search*
   www.dollsearcher.com
   doll collecting community with forums, search, links

*National Association of Antique Doll Dealers*
   www.nadda.org

*Our World of Dolls*
   www.our-world-of-dolls.com
   directory, search engine, and shops

*Theriault's*
   www.theriaults.com
   doll auctions, books, accessories, doll information

*United Federation of Doll Clubs*
   www.ufdc.org

## eBAY AND OTHER ONLINE AUCTIONS

*Auction Bytes*
 www.auctionbytes.com
 news and resources for the online auction community

*Auction Warehouse*
 www.auction-warehouse.com

*Bidville*
 www.bidville.com

*eBay*
 www.ebay.com


## ESTATE AND FINANCIAL PLANNING

*CFP Board of Standards*
 www.cfp.net
 referrals to Certified Financial Planners

*National Association of Financial and Estate Planning*
 www.nafep.com

*Nolo*
 www.nolo.com
 reference books and legal document templates


## FASHION

*Costume Gallery*
 www.costumegallery.com
 fashion library containing catalogs, photos, history

*Costumer's Manifesto*
 www.costumes.org

*Costume Society of America*
 www.costumesocietyamerica.com

*FashionDig*

www.fashiondig.com

news, shopping, fashion calendar, store locater, forums, chat, links

*Vintage Fashion Guild*

www.vintagefashionguild.org

online museum, labels database, forums, exhibits

## FURNITURE

*American Decorative Arts*

www.decorativearts.com

Modern furniture manufacturers and design resources, catalog reprints, links to other Modern information sites

*Carnegie Library*

www.carnegielibrary.org

look under "locations," music and art lists, for their "Researching Antique Furniture" page

*Connected Lines*

www.connectedlines.com

software download for furniture identification

*University of Delaware Library*

www.2lib.udel.edu

look for the Early American Antiques Web Resource page

## GOLD AND PRECIOUS METALS

*Kitco*

www.kitco.com

daily gold price quotes, articles, historical charts, analysis of gold and currencies

*GoldCentral.Com*

www.goldcentral.com

gold coin and rare coin dealer with free encyclopedia, market commentary, charts, news

*World Gold Council*
www.gold.org
information about investment, dealers, gold prices

## JEWELRY

*American Gem Society*
www.ags.org
locate a jeweler, gemologist or appraiser, ask an expert a question

*Gemological Institute of America*
www.gia.edu
information about gem grading, locate a gem laboratory

*International Gem Society*
www.gemsociety.org
information and educational services about gemstones

*Milky Way Jewels*
www.milkywayjewels.com
links to educational resources, club and newsletter, discussion groups, and reference materials

*National Jeweler*
www.nationaljeweler.com
online version of a magazine for jewelry professionals, auction results, market reports, news

*TimeZone*
www.timezone.com
information resources, forum, community, news for watch collectors

## MEMORABILIA

*America West Archives*
www.americawestarchives.com
Americana, Western, historical sales, analysis, authentication

*Beckett*
> www.beckett.com
> publishers of price guides and magazines on sports collectibles

*Collectors' Universe*
> www.collectors.com
> grading and authentication, links to affiliates

*Conway's Vintage Movie Posters & Autographs*
> www.autographsmovieposters.com

*Global Protection*
> www.globalprotection.com
> grading, authentication, consumer resources

*Learn about Movie Posters*
> www.learnaboutmovieposters.com
> auction news, links to poster dealers, info

*Primarily Petroliana*
> www.oldgas.com
> Gas Station memorabilia

*PSA, Professional Sports Authenticator*
> www.psa.com

*Railroadiana*
> www.railroadiana.org
> railroad memorabilia museum

*Vintage 429*
> www.vintage429.com
> historical, sports, Hollywood, autographs, music

## ONLINE SAFETY

*Scambusters*
> www.scambusters.org

*Wired Safety*
> www.wiredsafety.org

## PENS

Pentrace
    www.pentrace.com
    pen collecting community

The Vintage Pens Website
    www.vintagepens.com
    pen retailer with collecting resources

## PERIODICALS ONLINE

*Antiques and the Arts*
    www.antiquesandthearts.com

*Art and Antiques*
    www.artandantiques.net

*Maine Antique Digest*
    www.maineantiquedigest.com

## POSTCARDS

*Postcard Traders Association (UK)*
    www.postcard.co.uk

*San Francisco Bay Area Postcard Club*
    www.postcard.org

## REFERENCE BOOKS AND PRICE GUIDES

*JR's Collector Reference Books*
    www.jrsbooks.com

*New York Public Library Reference Guides*
    www.nypl.org/research/

*Robby's Bookshelf*
    www.robbysbookshelf.com

## RUGS

*Jozan Oriental Rug Portal*
> www.jozan.net
> articles, news, rug guide, rug directory, auction news

*Old Carpet.Com*
> www.oldcarpet.com
> rug dealer with identification guide, info, and FAQs about rugs

*RugMan*
> www.rugman.com
> rug dealer and importer with tutorials on Persian and Oriental rugs

## SILVER

*Online Encyclopedia of Silver*
> www.925-1000.com
> directory of silver marks, hallmarks, and maker's marks, question and
> answer forum

*Replacements Ltd.*
> www.replacements.com
> information and identification of silver patterns

*Silver Magazine*
> www.silvermag.com
> news, articles, profiles of manufacturers, patterns, book and price guide
> reviews, help with identifications

## STAMPS

*American Philatelic Society*
> www.stamps.org

*Ask Phil*
> www.askphil.org
> all-reference site sponsored by Collectors Club of Chicago

*Delcampe*
> www.delcampe.com
> auction site for stamps, postcards, old paper collections, other collectibles

*Find Your Stamps Value*
> www.findyourstampsvalue.com
> free trial search, subscription search, referrals

*Linn's*
> www.linns.com
> website of the world's largest weekly stamp newsletter

*Stamp Auction Results*
> www.stampauction.com

*Stamp Domain*
> www.stampdomain.com
> links to clubs, societies, auction info, country resources, postal history, stamp auctioneers

*Stamplink*
> www.stamplink.com
> "the world's hottest stamp collecting site" with links

## TOYS

*Action Figure Authority*
> www.toygrader.com
> action figure grading and archives

*All Info about Toys*
> www.toyscollectibles.allinfo-about.com
> the All Info site's toy section with links, books, toy news, blog

*Antique Toys.Com*
> www.antiquetoys.com
> glossary, toy history, links, info on manufacturers, appraisals

*Diecast Car Collectors Zone*
  www.diecast.org

*Gasoline Alley Antiques*
  www.gasolinealleyantiques.com
  dealers in toys, model railroads, nostalgia

*Lionel Railroad Collectors Club of America*
  www.lionelcollectors.org

*Lucky Bears*
  www.luckybears.com
  Teddy Bear history, manufacturers, identifying marks, prices

*National Model Railroad Association*
  www.nmra.com

*Toy Box 2000*
  www.toybox2000.com
  online classified ads for buying and selling toys, links

*The Toy Cars Collectors Association*
  www.toynutz.com

*Toyzine*
  www.toyzine.com
  toy auctions, dealer listings, price information, news

# INDEX